THE BEST RECIPES FROM
NEW MEXICO'S B&Bs

BY STEVE LARESE

New Mexico Magazine

THE BEST RECIPES FROM NEW MEXICO'S B&Bs

10 9 8 7 6 5 4 3 2 1 (Museum of New Mexico Press edition)

Author/Photographer: Steve Larese
Editors: Steve Larese, Andrew Collins, Christiane Lopez
Book Designer & Production Manager: Bette Brodsky

Cover photo: Green chile egg bake at the Old Taos Guesthouse, Taos
Title page photo: Dining room at Casa del Granjero, Albuquerque
Page ii photo: A quiet corner at Los Poblanos Inn, Albuquerque

Library of Congress Control Number: 2004110338
ISBN: 978-0-89013-600-3
Printed in Korea

Museum of New Mexico Press
P O Box 2087
Santa Fe, NM 87504
mnmpress.org

THE BEST RECIPES

TABLE OF CONTENTS

Poblanos Cazuelitas, P. 17

Pear Walnut Bread, P. 66

High Feather Balsamic, bonus recipe card

Orange Poppyseed Cake, P. 116

FOREWORD

The first time I stayed at a bed-and-breakfast, I was a little anxious. The thought of being a stranger in a stranger's home filled with a bunch of other strangers was not my idea of a relaxing vacation. Would I be expected to make witty chitchat while brushing my teeth? Would the innkeeper come in and rip the covers off me if I wanted to sleep past nine? Would harsh stares be cast my way if I came to breakfast in my socks?

Upon entering my room with its glowing kiva fireplace and private patio with a sweeping view of the purple Sangre de Cristos, any uncertainty melted away, along with any stress I had brought with me. Ever since, I've been addicted to b&bs and have come to cherish the views they offer, the comfort they provide and, above all, the people who lovingly operate them. Far from feeling like a stranger, I have made many friends with both owners and guests.

"It can be tough sometimes when people leave," says Nancy Leeson, who owns Casa de la Cuma in Santa Fe with her husband, Alex. "Everyone's tearing up at checkout, and you've just met these people a few days ago."

Often the owners of b&bs are as fascinating as the property and scenery. The Leesons had lucrative careers in New York at the time of September 11. After volunteering to help victims of the attacks, they decided to make a major life change and pursue their dream of running a bed-and-breakfast in New Mexico.

"We knew we needed to do something more human-oriented, more organic," Nancy says. "I can't think of a better way to connect with people than to bring them into your home and cook for them."

"You immediately see people enjoying your food fresh out of the oven," says Tim

Reeves, who has owned the Old Taos Guesthouse with his wife, Leslie, since 1989. "That's still exciting morning after morning, year after year. People choose us to provide for them the two things they cherish most—a sound sleep and a good meal. There's nothing more rewarding for us than to make people happy."

I wanted to share with you some of those recipes that have been making guests happy for years and asked b&bs from around the state to submit their favorites—the dishes and desserts that their guests request every stay. These tried-and-true recipes are intended to be quick and simple. They've been refined and perfected after hundreds of mornings and thousands of guests, and now more than 40 of New Mexico's best bed-and-breakfasts have graciously shared them. I hope you're able to re-create some of the nurturing charm of these properties in the comfort of your own kitchen. But be warned: Trying these recipes at home can lead to an extreme case of wanderlust. If you wish to visit some of these b&bs on your own (and I hope you do), see the contact information starting on page 125. For more information on New Mexico's bed-and-breakfasts, log on to www.nmbba.org or call the New Mexico Bed and Breakfast Association at 800-661-6649.

Keep in mind that some of the recipes were developed at a higher altitude (Santa Fe is almost 7,000 feet above sea level). Lower-altitude cooks may find that they need to adjust cooking times, temperatures and ingredient amounts.

And so I hope you devour this eclectic cookbook. I can only hope that these pages end up stained, stuck together and torn from use in your kitchen, and that the meals they help you make bring warmth and happiness to your family and friends. As any b&b owners will tell you, they're certainly not in the business for the money but rather to make friends out of strangers. Eat well, and know you have many friends throughout New Mexico.

—Steve Larese, December 2004

Please note: Some of the b&bs have closed or changed owners since this book's first printing.

SAVORY

Mountain Crepes, P. 38
From the Cimarron Rose B&B, Grants

Citrus-Marinated Shrimp, P. 11
From the Cinnamon Morning, Albuquerque

CITRUS-MARINATED SHRIMP

From the Cinnamon Morning, Albuquerque

1 cup freshly squeezed orange juice
$1/2$ cup freshly squeezed lemon juice
$1/2$ cup freshly squeezed key lime juice
$3/4$ cup ketchup
$1/4$ cup vodka
$1/4$ cup orange liqueur

$1/4$ t. hot pepper sauce
$1/4$ cup olive oil
1 small red onion, thinly sliced and diced
$1 1/2$ lbs. cooked, peeled large shrimp
   (24 pieces for 6 servings)
1 cup finely chopped cilantro (adjust
   to taste)

* Combine juices, ketchup, vodka, liqueur and pepper sauce in large bowl.
* Whisk in the oil.
* Add shrimp, onion and cilantro and mix well.
* Cover and refrigerate at least 3 hours and up to 6 hours.
* Drain before serving. Four shrimp skewered together makes a nice presentation.

Serves 6

ARTICHOKE & CHILE RAMEKIN

From the Brooks Street Inn, Taos

1½ cups grated kasseri cheese (can substitute Monterey Jack)

1 cup mayonnaise

4 to 6 oz. chopped canned or frozen green chiles

2 t. dried crushed red chile pepper

½ red or yellow bell pepper, chopped

1½ to 2 t. chopped fresh garlic

1½ cups chopped artichoke hearts (canned in water)

* Preheat oven to 350°F.
* Fold above ingredients together until mixed.
* Spray dish with Pam.
* Bake in oven for 25 to 35 minutes or until brown around the edges.
* Serve warm on slices of French baguette that have been coated with garlic butter and toasted in broiler.
* This is also very good served with blue corn tortilla chips.

Makes approximately 1½ quarts

ROSA'S CARNE ADOVADA

From Casa del Granjero, Albuquerque

20-30 red chile pods

3 whole allspice

3 whole cloves

2 large bay leaves

$1/8$ t. ground ginger

$1/4$ t. ground cumin

$1/2$ t. oregano leaves

$1/4$ t. rosemary

3 or 4 cloves of garlic

2 T. chicken base or broth

2 T. orange juice

4 to 5 lbs. pork loin, trimmed, and cut into
    bite-sized pieces

• Place 3 tablespoons or more of oil into a large stew pot. Lightly sauté the pork pieces for about 15 minutes. Set aside.

• Place chile pods in a large bowl and cover with very hot water, soak for 30 minutes. (Repeating the soaking and draining will lessen the heat of the chiles if desired.) Drain pods and remove seeds and stems and set aside. Place drained and cleaned pods in batches in a blender, about half full.

• Add broth or base with water to leave 2 inches of room from top of the blender. Add the spices and orange juice and blend until a paste is formed. Repeat process until all pods are used.

• When all batches are complete, pour into a large pan, add the meat and simmer for about 1 hour. If the liquid thickens too much, just add a little more broth or water.

CHILES RELLENOS CASSEROLE

From Casa del Granjero, Albuquerque

1 cup green chiles, roasted, peeled and chopped

2 eggs, slightly beaten

$1^1/_4$ cups sharp cheddar cheese, grated

$1^1/_4$ cups Monterey Jack cheese, grated

$1/_2$ cup flour

1 t. baking powder

$1 \, ^1/_2$ cups milk

$1/_2$ cup sour cream (garnish)

1 avocado, peeled, pitted and sliced (garnish)

1 cup salsa

• Preheat oven to 350°F.

• In a large bowl, mix first seven ingredients, stirring until well-incorporated.

• Place the mixture in a 10-inch buttered pie pan.

• Bake for 50 minutes, or until fully set.

• Remove from oven and let sit for 5 minutes.

• Cut into 6 pie-shaped wedges.

• Garnish each slice with sour cream and avocado slices.

• Serve salsa on the side.

Serves 6

CHILES QUILLAS YUCATÁN

From Casa del Granjero, Albuquerque

2 cups shredded cheddar cheese

15 corn tortillas, torn into pieces

vegetable oil for sautéing

1½ cups pork, beef, ham or chicken, cubed

1 medium onion, chopped

1 T. chopped garlic

chicken base or bouillon

1 cup chopped green chiles

1 cup tomatoes with juice

salt

dash oregano

dash cumin

* In a large skillet, sauté the corn tortillas until slightly crisp. Set aside.

* In another skillet, sauté the meat of your choice until cooked through, then add onion, garlic, tomatoes and green chiles, and salt, oregano and cumin to taste.

* Mix the base or bouillon with one cup of water and add to the meat mixture. Cook until liquid is slightly reduced, then add to the corn tortillas, mix well. Add water if necessary to make liquid level rise above the tortillas. It should be visible around the edge of the skillet.

* Let this mixture cook on low heat until it is all absorbed.

* Cover the surface with cheese and continue to cook an additional 2 to 3 minutes.

* Remove from heat, allow to cool and refrigerate. Spoon the mixture onto a pizza pan and cover and refrigerate. To serve, cut into approximate portions, heat in microwave for 2 minutes and serve with salsa.

Serves 8

CHILE-POTATO BAKE

From the Don Gaspar Inn, Santa Fe

1 large package of frozen hash brown potatoes

3 cups of grated Jack/cheddar cheese combo

2 cups of mild diced frozen green chiles, thawed or fresh roasted and peeled

12 eggs

$2/3$ cup half-and-half

$1/2$ t. of garlic powder

1 t. of salt

* Sprinkle frozen hash brown potatoes over the bottom of a 9-by-13-inch baking pan sprayed with Pam.

* Spread half of the grated cheese mixture over the potatoes. Spread half of the diced chiles over the cheese and repeat another layer.

* Preheat the oven to 375°F.

* Beat the eggs with the half-and-half, garlic powder, and salt and pour over potato mixture.

* Bake for 45 to 50 minutes or until the center is cooked through.

* Remove from the oven and let sit for 5 minutes before cutting into squares.

* Serve with fresh salsa and warm tortillas.

Serves 15

POBLANOS CAZUELITAS

From Los Poblanos Inn, Albuquerque

4 eggs

1½ cups thick cream

½ t. salt

1½ cups grated Monterey Jack or medium-sharp cheddar cheese

2 large poblanos chiles, roasted, peeled, seeded and sliced

• Preheat oven to 350°F.

• In a mixing bowl beat the eggs with a fork, adding the cream and salt a little at a time.

• Divide the cheese evenly among 6 *cazuelitas* (ramekins).

• Top with chile slices and fill with the egg mixture.

• Place the cazuelitas in a larger shallow pan, filled halfway with hot water and bake for 45 minutes or until set, to create a custard texture.

Serves 6

TAOS GREEN CHILE EGG BAKE

From the Old Taos Guesthouse, Taos

2 cups frozen hash browns

1 cup croutons

$1^1/_2$ cups grated cheddar cheese

1 cup bacon bits

10 organic eggs

$1^1/_2$ cup chopped green chiles, hot

2 cups milk

The night before:

* Spray a 9-by-13-inch baking pan.
* Layer the dry ingredients in order of hash browns, croutons, cheddar cheese and bacon.
* Separately beat the eggs with milk and add the green chile.
* Pour this mix evenly over the layers. Refrigerate.

In the morning:

* Preheat oven to 350°F and bake for one hour.
* Let it cool a little before cutting and serving.

Serves 8 to 12

SPANISH EGGS
From Casa Escondida B&B, Chimayó

8 eggs, beaten
1/2 cup chopped onion (red onion is best)
1/2 cup chopped *nopalitos* (canned prickly pear cactus)
1/3 cup shredded cheddar cheese
1 T. prepared chopped garlic (less if you are using fresh garlic)
2 t. red chile powder (eggs should turn slightly pink in color when blended with
the chile powder)
splash of half-and-half or milk
salt and black pepper to taste
cilantro, dried or fresh, for garnish

* Blend all of the ingredients except cilantro.
* Scramble the egg mixture in a sauté pan until almost dry. Then top with additional cheddar cheese. Turn off the heat.
* Cover the skillet to melt the cheese.
* Slide the cooked eggs onto a serving plate.
* Garnish with some dollops of salsa and sprinkle with cilantro.
* Serve with warm flour tortillas.
* The eggs can be eaten as is, or rolled-up in a warm tortilla to make breakfast burritos. Salsa and sour cream can be used to dress the breakfast burritos.

Serves 4

GREEN CHILE TORTE
From Alma del Monte, Taos

4 eggs

1½ cups milk

½ t. black pepper

3 10-inch flour tortillas

2 cups grated Monterey Jack cheese

¾ cup grated medium cheddar cheese

13 oz. frozen green chiles, mild

½ cup finely chopped ham or bacon (optional)

* In blender, mix eggs, milk and black pepper.

* Spray 10-inch quiche pan or 10-inch pie plate with Pam. Place one tortilla in pan.

* Mix cheeses and chiles together; spread ⅓ of mixture on tortilla.

* Repeat the layering process with 2 more tortillas and remainder of cheese/chile mixture.

* Pour egg mixture over tortillas. Sprinkle ham or bacon on top.

* Refrigerate overnight. Bake at 350°F for 45 minutes, then 250°F for 15 minutes.

* Let stand 5 minutes, cut into wedges, garnish and serve.

Serves 6 to 8

GIGI'S CHILE CON QUESO OMELET

From the Grant Corner Inn, Santa Fe

1 medium onion, chopped

1 clove garlic, minced

2 T. butter, divided

1 16-oz. can whole tomatoes,
   drained and chopped

1 4-oz. can chopped green chiles, drained

1 T. all-purpose flour

$1/2$ cup half-and-half

salt and cayenne pepper to taste

1 cup shredded mild cheddar cheese

12 eggs

chopped cilantro and jalapeño
   slices for garnish

* Sauté onion and garlic in 1 tablespoon butter.

* Add flour and stir over medium heat 4 minutes.

* Gradually add half-and-half, stirring until mixture is smooth and thick. Season to taste with salt and cayenne.

* Handful by handful, add the cheese, stirring between additions to smooth.

* To make the chile con queso, stir the tomatoes and chiles into the cheese blend, cover and set aside.

* For each omelet, pour $1/4$ of beaten egg mixture into seasoned omelet pan over medium-high heat.

* Let set 1 minute, then lift edges all around, allowing uncooked egg to run underneath.

* Fill each omelet with chile con queso, fold in half and transfer to serving plate. Top with more chile con queso, chopped cilantro and jalapeño slices.

21

EGGS DEL SOL
From Hacienda del Sol, Taos

1 4-oz. can of green chiles
½ cup flour
7 to 8 eggs, slightly beaten
1½ cups cottage cheese
2 cups Monterey Jack cheese, grated
2 cups cheddar cheese, grated
½ cup salsa
1 t. baking powder

* Lightly grease 9½-by-11-inch pan.
* Pour green chiles lightly over pan.
* Mix all the other ingredients together in a large bowl.
* Pour mixture over green chiles.
* Wrap and store in refrigerator overnight.
* Preheat oven to 350°F.
* Place small pan in a large pan, filled with 1 inch of water.
* Bake casserole for 1 hour, or until set.

Serves 6 to 8

CHILAQUILES

From the Cottonwood Inn, Taos

Tomato chile sauce

Place the following ingredients in a blender:

28-oz. can of diced tomatoes

1 or 2 jalapeño chiles, stemmed

$1/2$ of a small white or yellow onion

1 or 2 large cloves of garlic

12 to 15 sprigs of fresh cilantro

* Blend until well-mixed, then fry in 1 tablespoon of vegetable oil over medium-high heat.
* After about 5 minutes the sauce should have thickened. Set aside, or refrigerate overnight.

Chilaquiles mixture

In a bowl combine:

8 eggs, scrambled

$1/2$ cup grated melting cheese, such as asadero or Monterey Jack

* Set aside 6 corn tortillas (cut into wedges) or $1 1/2$ cups tortilla chips.
* In a large frying pan, add vegetable oil and the egg-cheese mixture.
* When the eggs start to set, add the tomato chile sauce and tortillas or chips.
* Mix well and continue to fry briefly until ingredients are heated through, but the tortillas or chips are still crunchy.
* Serve immediately.

Serves 6 to 8

GREEN CHILE & CHEESE FRITTATA

From Rancho Manzana, Chimayó

5 eggs

1 cup chopped roasted green chiles–if using frozen chiles, drain off all liquid

1 cup grated Monterey Jack cheese

1 T. butter

pinch of salt

tomato and cilantro for garnish

* Preheat oven to 400°F.

* Separate eggs and beat the whites until stiff but not dry.

* Fold in the yolks, then the cheese, chile and salt.

* Heat a cast-iron skillet over medium heat.

* Grease the skillet and heat again until butter sizzles but does not burn.

* Put ingredients in skillet, and bake for 30 minutes or until lightly browned and the center is firm.

* Let frittata sit in skillet for 3 to 4 minutes and then slide onto a plate.

* Garnish with tomato rounds and cilantro. Serve warm or at room temperature.

Serves 6

SPINACH CHEESE ENCHILADAS
with poached eggs

From the Bobcat Inn, Santa Fe

Filling

1 cup cottage cheese

1 cup cheddar cheese, grated

1 cup Monterey Jack cheese, grated

$1/2$ cup chopped black olives

3 small jalepeño peppers, chopped fine

salt and black pepper

• Combine ingredients for filling and set aside.

Spinach chile sauce

1 onion chopped

2 cups roasted or frozen green chiles, mild

$1/2$ t. garlic

1 8-oz pkg. frozen chopped spinach, puréed

2 T. flour

2 T. vegetable oil

2 cups vegetable stock

$1/2$ t. salt

1 T. cumin

1 t. oregano

1 t. red chile powder

• Sauté onion and garlic in oil. Cook until onion is transparent. Add flour and brown slightly.

• Add stock slowly, stirring constantly. Add chile, spinach and seasonings.

• For enchiladas, dip corn tortillas into hot vegetable oil to soften and drain on paper towels.

• Roll tortillas with filling (2 to 3 tablespoons of filling). Large ones are better.

• Top with sauce and grated cheddar and Jack cheese.

• Bake at 350°F for 30 minutes in a greased casserole. Do not cover.

• Serve with poached egg, salsa and sour cream.

GINGER SALMON
From the Adobe Nido B&B, Albuquerque

1-inch or thicker salmon fillet per serving
1 T. minced ginger
1 T. finely chopped scallions
2 T. sesame soy sauce
2 to 3 T. of peanut oil

* Mix the ginger, scallions and soy sauce in a bowl and set aside.
* Poach salmon fillet in water in a shallow pan. Use lid to keep it moist.
* In a small skillet, heat peanut oil to the point of smoking.
* While oil is heating, put poached salmon on a serving plate and top with ginger mixture.
* When oil is hot, drizzle over the ginger-topped salmon; it should sizzle. Serve immediately; asparagus makes an excellent side.

Serves 1 per salmon fillet

DEEP-DISH BREAKFAST PIZZA
Chicago-style
From Alma del Monte, Taos

12 oz. regular pork sausage

6 oz. hot pork sausage

1 package refrigerated crescent roll dough (8 count)

2 hash brown potato patties, thawed

5 eggs, beaten

2 cups shredded cheddar cheese

* Sauté sausage in skillet until brown and crumbly, drain.
* Pat roll dough into lightly greased deep-dish pizza pan (or quiche pan) sealing rolls together.
* Sprinkle crumbled potato patties and sausage over dough.
* Pour eggs over top.
* Sprinkle with cheese.
* Bake at 350°F for 30 to 40 minutes.

Serves 6 to 8

STUFFED EGGPLANT

From the Bear Mountain Lodge, Silver City

4 medium eggplants

salt to taste

10 T. extra virgin olive oil

2 medium-size onions, cut lengthwise
    and thinly sliced

6 large cloves, chopped

1/2 lb. ripe tomatoes, peeled, seeded
    and chopped

1/4 cup finely chopped fresh parsley leaves

1/4 t. cinnamon

1 t. sugar

2 T. fresh lemon juice

1/4 cup water

• Cut each eggplant in half lengthwise. Make a deep lengthwise slit along the flesh side of the eggplant, making sure you don't puncture the skin. Salt the flesh and set aside, flesh-side down, on some paper towels for 30 minutes to leach the eggplant of its bitter juices. Dry with paper towels.

• In a large skillet, heat 4 tablespoons of the olive oil over high heat; once it's smoking, fry the eggplant, flesh-side down, until golden brown, about 4 minutes. Remove from the skillet to drain on some paper towels.

• In the same skillet, add the remaining 6 tablespoons olive oil and heat over medium-high heat, then cook the onions and garlic until soft and yellow, about 5 minutes, stirring frequently. Transfer the onions and garlic to a medium-sized bowl and mix well with the tomatoes, parsley, cinnamon, sugar, salt to taste and a few tablespoons of the cooking oil.

• Arrange the eggplant halves in a large skillet or casserole with the slit-side up. Gently open the slits so that the stuffing fills the slits and is spread to cover all the flesh. Sprinkle the lemon juice over the eggplant. Pour any remaining sauce or juices, along with the water, into the skillet, cover, and cook over low heat until the eggplant is soft, about 50 minutes, adding water to the skillet if it is getting too dry. Let the eggplant cool in the skillet and serve whole at room temperature or warm.

PEAR GINGER PANCAKES

From The Madeleine Inn, Santa Fe

1 cup flour
1 T. sugar
1 t. baking powder
$1/2$ t. baking soda
dash of salt
1 cup buttermilk
2 T. vegetable oil

1 egg, beaten
$1/2$ t. cinnamon
$1/4$ t. cardamom
$1/2$ t. finely minced or crystallized
    ginger
$1/2$ pear, peeled and cored

* Combine first 6 ingredients in bowl.
* Combine beaten egg with oil in separate bowl, add to first bowl, mix well.
* To the batter add cinnamon and remaining ingredients. Mix well.
* Pour onto hot griddle.

Makes 8 to 10 silver dollar-size pancakes

TOFU STIR-FRY & PANFRIED NOODLES

From Casa de la Cuma, Santa Fe

3 T. + 2 T. peanut oil

1 T. + 1 T. hot sesame oil

3 T. + 1 T. crushed garlic

3 T. + 2 T. red curry paste

$1/8$ cup + $1/4$ cup soy sauce

3 T. + 1 T. Memmi Soup Base

1 pack hard, spiced tofu, cubed

2 bunches scallions, chopped

1 package fresh shiitake mushrooms

1 package Hong Kong panfry noodles

2 eggs, lightly scrambled

30 leaves basil, chopped

• Boil noodles for 15 seconds. Drain and set aside.

• Preheat wok to medium high. Prepare wok with first 6 ingredients (hold second measurement for later).

• Sauté scallions for 1 minute.

• Add tofu and mushrooms. Sauté for 3 minutes.

• Create a "hole" in center of ingredients in wok and pour eggs into it, swirling slowly. When eggs start to set, gently swirl them into remaining mixture. Set aside mixture in warm bowl.

• Prepare wok again with remaining measurements of first 6 ingredients.

• Pan fry noodles, tossing with tongs until coated and slightly browned. Turn heat off and add other ingredients, tossing with tongs until mixed.

• Add basil leaves and transfer to large serving bowl.

Serves 4

CHICKEN SKEWERS
with orange-chipotle sauce
From the Four Kachinas Inn, Santa Fe

2 lbs. of chicken breast cut into 1-inch wide, thin strips
1½ cups orange-chipotle mustard sauce (recipe follows)

Orange-chipotle mustard sauce

1 6 oz. can of frozen orange juice

3 T. chipotle chiles

2 T. honey

2 T. Dijon mustard

1 t. minced garlic

⅓ cup chopped fresh cilantro, packed

3 T. fresh lime juice

½ t. salt

2 T. vegetable oil

* Place all the sauce ingredients in a food processor or blender and purée until smooth; set aside.
* "Thread" chicken strips onto skewers in a long ribbon fashion. Grill or broil chicken skewers until meat is fully cooked.
* Place cooked skewers into large glass baking pan. Pour the orange-chipotle mustard over the skewers and toss until coated. Serve warm.
* Lamb, shrimp, scallops or pork can be substituted for the chicken.

Serves 6

CHORIZO ROLL

From Hacienda Vargas, Algodones

6 eggs, beaten

3/4 cup milk

1 cup cheddar cheese

2 links Mexican chorizo, cooked and drained

1 cup French bread, cubed

4 oz. cream cheese, softened and creamed

* Combine beaten eggs, milk, cheddar cheese, chorizo and cubed bread.
* Spray a 9-by-13-inch jelly pan with Pam, line the jelly pan with foil (including the sides) and spray generously with Pam.
* Spread the mixture into the pan.
* Bake at 350°F for 20 to 25 minutes until firm to touch. Let cool.
* Turn out onto wax paper and spread cream cheese on entire surface.
* Carefully roll tightly, peeling the foil off as you go and using it as a helper.
* Slice and garnish with avocado.

Serves 4

SCRAMBLED EGGS
with smoked salmon & cream cheese
From the Little Tree B&B, Taos

2 farm eggs

¼ cup milk

salt and black pepper to taste

½ T. butter

6 to 7 small pieces of smoked salmon

full-fat cream cheese

dill for garnish

* Break eggs into a small bowl and whisk them with milk (add more if necessary and season with salt and pepper).
* Melt butter over medium heat in a small omelet pan.
* Once butter sizzles, add 6 to 7 small pieces of smoked salmon.
* Stir, then add eggs. Watch carefully.
* As soon as eggs come together and have lost most of their liquidity, turn off heat and pinch small fingernail-sized portions of cream cheese into the eggs—about 5 to 7 lumps.
* Lightly toss.
* Serve and garnish with fresh dill.

Serves 1

MACARONI & CHEESE
with chipotle garlic cheese breadcrumbs

From Casa de la Cuma, Santa Fe

For bread crumbs:

2 T. unsalted butter

2 T. olive oil

4 large garlic cloves, finely chopped

1 cup coarse fresh bread crumbs

1 cup mashed CHEEZE-IT White
   Cheddar crackers

For Casserole:

7 T. chopped chipotle chiles in adobo

4 T. unsalted butter

$1/4$ cup all-purpose flour

3 cups whole milk

2 cups heavy cream

1 T. dry mustard

$1/4$ T. cayenne pepper or to taste

15 drops Tabasco or to taste

1 lb. macaroni

2 lbs. extra-sharp white cheddar, grated

To make bread crumbs:

* Heat butter and oil in a 10-inch heavy skillet over medium heat until foam subsides.

* Cook garlic bread crumbs and crackers, stirring, until crumbs are browned.

* Drain oil on paper towels, and season lightly with salt.

To make casserole:

* Preheat oven to 350°F.

* Melt butter in a saucepan over moderate heat. Add flour and cook, whisking, 1 minute.

34

- Whisk in milk, cream, and mustard. Simmer, whisking, for 3 minutes, making a white sauce.
- Cook macaroni in a 6-quart pot of boiling salted water until just tender.
- Drain in colander and transfer to a large bowl. Stir in white sauce, cheese, and salt to taste.
- Fill a 1$\frac{1}{2}$-quart casserole pan with macaroni mixture.
- Stir chipotles into macaroni. Sprinkle with bread crumbs.
- Bake casserole 30 minutes or until bubbly.

GEORGE'S BREAKFAST ENCHILADA

From The Madeleine Inn, Santa Fe

6 flour tortillas, cut into small pieces
1 cup ham
2 cups grated cheese
1 zucchini, diced

10 eggs
3 cups prepared green chile sauce
salt and black pepper to taste

- Spray a 13-by-9-by-2-inch pan with Pam.
- Line bottom of pan with tortilla pieces.
- Layer ham, cheese and zucchini.
- Beat eggs and add green chile sauce to egg mixture. Pour over other ingredients in pan.
Top with cheese.
- Let stand overnight in refrigerator.
- Bake at 375°F for 45 minutes or until top is browned and puffy.

BAKED BRIE

From the Water Street Inn, Santa Fe

1 14-oz. round Brie
1 package large size refrigerated biscuit dough
1/4 cup brown sugar
1/4 cup sliced almonds
1 pear, sliced vertically in 1/4-inch widths
sesame seeds

• Preheat oven to 375°F.

• Combine and roll out 6 of the biscuits into a round pie shape.

• In the center place almonds, brown sugar and pears, in that order.

• Place Brie round on top and fold biscuit dough around, pinching together at the center.

• Turn over and place on baking sheet.

• Brush dough with olive oil and sprinkle with sesame seeds.

• Place remaining two biscuits on pan to gauge doneness.

• Bake until well-browned. Serve warm.

SPINACH & CHEESE SQUARES

From the Water Street Inn, Santa Fe

2 T. butter

3 eggs

1 cup flour

1 cup milk

1 t. salt

1 t. baking powder

$1/2$ t. red pepper flakes

$1/2$ lb. grated cheddar cheese

$1/2$ lb. grated Monterey Jack cheese

$1/2$ cup chopped mushrooms

4 cups chopped, fresh spinach

1 diced red bell pepper

• Melt butter in a 9-by-13-inch pan.

• Beat eggs.

• Add flour, milk, salt and baking powder.

• Add pepper flakes, cheeses, mushrooms, spinach and bell pepper, mixing well.

• Spread into pan and bake at 350°F for 35 minutes.

• Cool 30 minutes before serving.

• Cut into squares.

MOUNTAIN CREPES
with cranberry-orange sauce

From the Cimarron Rose B&B, Grants

To make the crepes:

3 eggs (free-range)

$1^1/_3$ cups milk

2 T. melted butter

salt

1 cup unbleached flour

* In mixing bowl, beat the eggs and add milk. With hand mixer, gradually add the flour.
* Add melted butter.
* Lightly butter a skillet over moderate heat on the stove.
* Lift the pan away from heat and pour $1/_2$ cup of the batter into the skillet using a circular motion of the wrist and rotating the pan as needed to cover the bottom evenly.
* Cook the crepe until it bubbles through and is lightly browned on the bottom. Crepes are thicker, more rustic and substantial than traditional ones and will need to be flipped over and cooked for a short time longer. They should be soft but not sticky.
* Place on a warmed plate and cover with foil while pouring your next crepe into the pan.
* Spoon the sauce (recipe follows) over the crepe on the plate and either stack flat with sauce between each (great for a group of guests to cut into wedges like a cake) or fold into thirds and overlap on the plate. Garnish with orange twists or slices.

To make quick Cranberry-Orange Sauce:

1 cup sugar

2 T. cornstarch

1 can whole-berry cranberry sauce

2 cups water

$1/_4$ cup butter

zest and juice of 1 small orange

- Combine the sugar and cornstarch in medium saucepan using wire whisk to mix well.
- Gradually add the water and stir to eliminate lumps. Cook over medium heat until the sauce bubbles and thickens to a desired consistency–then remove from heat.
- Add the butter, cranberry sauce, and orange.

Note: Alternatively you can make a delicious lemon sauce using zest and juice from $1^1/_2$ lemons.

OVEN-BAKED OMELET

From the Country Club B&B, Roswell

8 eggs (well-beaten)

1 cup milk

2 cups grated cheese (Four Cheeses Mexican Blend)

1 cup diced ham

chopped green chiles to taste (about $1/_2$ cup)

- Mix all ingredients together.
- Pour into an 8-inch square dish sprayed with Pam.
- Bake at 350°F for 35 to 40 minutes, or until center is firm.

STUFFED FRENCH TOAST
with apricot glaze
From the Brooks Street Inn, Taos

1 8-oz. package cream cheese

1 t. almond extract

½ cup slivered almonds

1 loaf unsliced sourdough bread

4 eggs

½ cup half-and-half

½ cup milk

¾ t. vanilla

¾ t. cinnamon, to taste

½ t. nutmeg

1 12-oz. jar apricot preserves

1 16-oz. can apricots, drained

* In a small bowl, combine the cream cheese and the almond extract until fluffy.
* Stir in the nuts.
* Cut the bread into ¾-inch slices, then make a cut (about 2 inches long) on the bottom of each piece of bread. It needs to be large enough to create a pocket that will hold about 1 teaspoon of the cream cheese mixture. Stuff in the cream cheese mixture.
* Beat together the eggs, half-and-half, milk, vanilla and cinnamon. Dip the stuffed bread into the egg mixture and allow it to get thoroughly moist but not heavily soaked. Cook the bread on lightly greased griddle until golden.
* Heat the preserves, slice the apricots into thirds and add to the preserves with the nutmeg.
* Drizzle over the cooked toast.

Serves 6 to 8

BANANA FRENCH TOAST
with caramel topping

From the Wildflower B&B, Angel Fire

2 whole eggs

1/4 cup milk

1/2 t. cinnamon

1/2 t. nutmeg

2 whole bananas

6 thick slices of French bread (1 inch)

* Place all ingredients except bread and one banana into blender until smooth.
* Pour in flat dish or pie plate. Soak bread on both sides and grill both sides.

Caramel topping:

1/2 cup brown sugar

1/4 cup half-and-half

1/4 cup light corn syrup

2 T. margarine or butter

1 t. vanilla

2 to 3 T. pecan halves, or to taste

1 or 2 sliced bananas, or to taste

* Mix brown sugar, half-and-half, corn syrup, margarine or butter and vanilla in saucepan.
* Heat to a boil, stirring occasionally.
* Remove from heat, gently stir in pecans and banana slices.
* Stir until coated and serve over the French toast.

Serves 6

PUMPKIN PANCAKES

From Hacienda Vargas, Algodones

1 cup pumpkin purée

1 can evaporated milk

2 eggs

2 T. vegetable oil

2 T. brown sugar

1 t. vanilla

1 t. allspice

1 t. cinnamon

2 cups Bisquick

toasted pine nuts

* Combine all ingredients except nuts. Mix well.
* Pour batter on medium hot griddle and sprinkle with nuts.
* Turn when dry around edges and starting to bubble.

Makes approximately 16 pancakes

RANCH HOUSE PANCAKES

From High Feather Ranch, Cerrillos

3/4 cup flour
1/2 t. salt
1 t. sugar
1/4 t. baking soda
4 eggs, beaten
1 cup sour cream
1 cup cottage cheese
1 T. of vanilla

* Stir together dry ingredients.
* In separate bowl, whisk eggs until frothy then add sour cream, cottage cheese and vanilla.
* Add dry ingredients to egg mixture.
* Ladle onto hot griddle. You can make 4 or so large pancakes and stack them and cut into pie wedges.
* Serve with maple syrup.

Serves 4

BLUEBERRY-STUFFED FRENCH TOAST

From the Lazy K Ranch, Edgewood

12 slices French bread cut into cubes

2 8-oz. packages cream cheese cut into cubes

1 cup blueberries (can use frozen)

12 eggs

1/2 cup maple syrup

2 cups milk

1 t. vanilla

1 t. cinnamon

Syrup:

1 cup sugar

2 T. corn starch

1 cup water

1 cup blueberries

1 T. butter

* Grease 13-by-9-inch baking dish.

* Place half of the bread cubes in pan, scatter cream cheese cubes and blueberries over bread.

* Put remaining bread on top.

* Combine eggs, maple syrup, milk, cinnamon, and vanilla. Pour mixture evenly over bread.

* Cover with foil and chill overnight.

* Bake at 350°F for 30 minutes.

* Remove the foil and bake 30 minutes more.

* For the syrup, mix all and heat, dissolving ingredients completely.

Serves 10

FRENCH TOAST SOUFFLÉ

From the Old Taos Guesthouse, Taos

10 cups cubed raison-cinnamon bread
1 8-oz. block of cream cheese
8 large eggs
$1^1/_2$ cups milk
$^2/_3$ cup half-and-half
$^1/_2$ cup maple syrup
$^1/_2$ t. vanilla extract

• Place bread cubes in a 9-by-13-inch sprayed baking dish.

• Beat cream cheese with a mixer adding eggs one at a time. Beat until creamy. Add milk, half-and-half, maple syrup and vanilla, and mix until smooth.

• Pour egg mix over the cubed bread, cover and refrigerate overnight.

• In the morning, uncover and sprinkle with chopped pecans.

• Bake at 350°F for one hour.

• Let stand for 10 minutes and serve with real maple syrup.

Serves 12

PUFFED PANCAKES
with berry compote

From the Bear Mountain Lodge, Silver City

3 eggs

1 cup milk

1 cup flour

1 T. sugar

1/2 t. vanilla

pinch of salt

3 T. butter

powdered sugar

* Preheat oven to 350°F.
* Place first 6 ingredients in a blender and blend until smooth. It is important to use a blender as the pancake will puff up better when cooked.
* Heat a cast-iron skillet over medium heat.
* Add butter, being careful to coat sides and bottom of skillet.
* Put batter in skillet and cook for 30 minutes or until puffed up (about 4 inches) and lightly browned on the sides.
* Transfer to a plate, sprinkle with powdered sugar and serve immediately.

For the berry compote:

1 cup frozen raspberries

1 cup frozen blueberries

1 cup sugar

* Heat until hot and sugar dissolves. Pour onto pancake and serve warm.

ORGANIC POTATO PANCAKES

From Riversong Ranch, Taos

4 to 5 large potatoes

1 large onion

$1/4$ cup of flour

2 eggs

1 T. horseradish

1 t. salt

$1/2$ cup of sour cream (or soy sour cream)

1 t. of dried ground green chile powder

2 T. of ghee (clarified butter) or Spectrum organic shortening

• Peel and grate the potatoes on the fine sharp edge of the grater, so it will make a batter.

• Grate onion.

• Add eggs.

• Add the flour to absorb the water in the mixture.

• Add the rest of the ingredients except for the ghee.

• Mix by hand until it is well-blended. (If the batter is too liquid, add a little more flour. Test one pancake first.)

• Use the ghee in the frying pan. It is better than butter as it does not burn as easily. Fry until they are crispy.

• Serve with sour cream or apple sauce.

Makes 6 to 8 pancakes

BAKED WELSH RAREBIT

From Alma del Monte, Taos

1 cup grated strong cheddar cheese

1 T. butter

1/2 cup milk

1/2 t. salt

1/2 t. dry mustard

1/4 t. paprika

1/2 t. Worcestershire sauce

2 eggs

6 slices bread

* Beat butter, milk, salt, mustard, paprika, Worcestershire and eggs together until well-mixed.
* Stir in grated cheese.
* Butter bread slices. Cut in half to form triangles and arrange butter side down to cover the bottom of a shallow pie plate. Start with a star pattern with the triangles and then fill in.
* Pour cheese mixture over all. Bake at 400°F for 25 minutes.
* Garnish with meat, tomatoes, sour cream and guacamole.

Serves 2

DIEGO QUICHE

From High Feather Ranch, Cerrillos

$1/4$ cup melted butter

10 eggs, beaten

$1/2$ cup flour

1 t. baking powder

$1/2$ cup diced green chiles

1 lb. grated Swiss cheese

2 cups cottage cheese

$1/2$ cup sliced green onion (include the tops)

$1/2$ cup quartered cherry tomatoes

* Mix together the butter, eggs, flour and baking powder.
* Add rest of ingredients and mix all together.
* Pour into greased 9-by-13-inch casserole pan and bake at 400°F for 15 minutes, then at 350°F for 60 minutes.
* Cut into 8 servings and garnish with a dollop of sour cream and a sprig of fresh cilantro or basil.
* Serve with grilled asparagus, fried green tomatoes, warm tortillas and sausage or bacon.
* This crustless quiche may be made the night before and refrigerated for the morning.

Serves 8

BLUEBERRY BLINTZ SOUFFLE

From the Cottonwood Inn, Taos

Batter ingredients:

1 1/2 cups sour cream

1/2 cup orange juice

6 eggs

1/4 cup margarine, softened

1 cup flour

1/3 cup sugar

2 t. cinnamon

* In a blender, combine the above ingredients and blend well, occasionally scraping blender sides.

Filling ingredients:

16 oz. small-curd cottage cheese

2 egg yolks

1 T. sugar

1 t. vanilla extract

8 oz. cream cheese

1/2 cup fresh or frozen blueberries

* Except for the blueberries, mix above ingredients.
* Pour 1/2 batter into a greased 9-by-13-inch pan.
* Drop filling by spoonfuls into the batter, then sprinkle in 1/2 cup of blueberries.
* Pour remaining batter over the top.
* Bake at 350°F for 50 to 65 minutes, until puffed and golden brown.
* Cut and serve portions topped with blueberry sauce (recipe follows).

Blueberry Sauce:

2 cups blueberries (fresh or frozen)

1 cup water

1 cup sugar

2 T. cornstarch

1 T. butter

• In a small saucepan, combine water, sugar, cornstarch, and 1 cup of blueberries. Cook until the sauce thickens, stirring frequently. Mix in the remaining blueberries and butter.

TOSTADO QUICHE

From the Wildflower B&B, Angel Fire

1 flour tortilla

$1/3$ cup cheddar cheese, grated

$1/2$ t. red chile powder

1 T. scallions

1 T. ripe olives, sliced

1 T. green chiles

2 whole eggs

$1/2$ cup 2-percent lowfat milk

dash of salt

dash of dry mustard

• Warm tortilla in a dry, hot skillet and carefully fit into an ungreased $1^1/2$-cup ramekin, or other oven-safe bowl.

• Sprinkle with chile powder, cheese, onions and olives.

• Beat eggs, add milk, green chile, salt and mustard and pour over cheese in ramekin.

• Bake at 350°F for 30 minutes, or until set.

CALABACITAS FRITTATA

From El Paradero, Santa Fe

3 ears of corn on the cob
(or 1/2 cup frozen corn, thawed)
salt
1/2 medium onion
1/2 cup olive oil
2 small zucchinis, cubed into small pieces

15 eggs
1 cup grated Monterey Jack cheese
1/2 t. pepper
1 t. dried basil
1/2 t. dried thyme

* Scrape corn off of cob and toss in 3 tablespoons of olive oil. Put on baking sheet lined with aluminum foil. Sprinkle with 1/2 t. salt.
* Roast at 400 °F for about 15 minutes, or until some kernels have turned light brown.
* Reduce oven temperature to 350°F.
* Sauté onion in remaining olive oil in a skillet (approximately 11-inches across) with an ovenproof handle until soft.
* Add squash and zucchinis and sauté until soft. Add corn.
* Beat eggs, salt, basil, pepper, and thyme, and pour into skillet. Turn heat to low.
* Add grated cheese.
* Cook on stove until barely set on bottom (about 5 minutes).
* Put in oven and cook for 15 to 20 minutes, or until set. Let sit for a few minutes before serving.

Serves 8

GRANDMA TINA'S BELINAS
From Hacienda Manzanal, Corrales

1 package yeast

3¼ cups warm water

3½ cups flour

2 eggs, beaten

⅓ cup sugar

1 t. salt

1 t. baking powder

• Dissolve yeast in ¼ cup warm water. Alternate flour and rest of water. Let this mixture stand overnight, or about 4 hours.

• Add the remaining ingredients. If mixture is too thick, use warm milk to thin. It should be fairly thin so it will pour easily.

• Heat and lightly grease a skillet. Pour in enough batter to cover bottom of skillet. Use about ½ dipper of batter for each pancake. Cook on medium-high heat.

• Bake until bubbles form and belina is brown on one side. Turn and cook until brown on other side.

• Spread 2 belinas with butter and syrup, then roll up using the tine of the fork.

Serves 6

CACTUS QUICHE
From the Cimarron Rose B&B, Grants

4 breakfast veggie patties

5 scallions

¼ sweet red bell pepper

1 cup *nopalitos* (canned prickly pear cactus)

2 T. diced roasted green chiles

¾ cup Monterey Jack cheese

3 eggs (free-range)

1 cup half-and-half

1 cup heavy cream

salt and black pepper to taste

fresh plum tomato and cilantro for garnish

* In a heavy skillet, brown the veggie patties in butter, breaking them into small bite-size pieces, and set aside.
* Rinse the cactus and drain well.
* In same skillet, sauté the onions and red bell pepper in olive oil until tender. Add cactus and chile to heat through and release flavors. Remove from heat.
* In mixing bowl, beat the eggs. Add half-and-half and cream, salt and pepper to taste.
* Cover the bottom of your crust (recipe follows) with the crumbled veggie patties.
* Add some cheese, then the red bell pepper and cactus mixture and remaining cheese.
* Pour the creamy egg mixture over the top.
* Place in 350°F oven for 1 hour or until knife inserted in center comes out clean.
* Let stand for 10 minutes before cutting.
* Garnish with chopped plum tomatoes on top and fresh sprig of cilantro.
* This dish goes especially well with either sliced melon or papaya.

Press-in Pie Crust

$1/2$ cup unbleached flour
$1/2$ cup whole-wheat flour
$1/3$ cup butter
buttermilk

* In mixing bowl, cut the butter into the flour with pastry cutter.
* Add enough buttermilk so that dough is workable but not wet or sticky.
* Knead 5 times or so.
* Place dough ball in the center of your pastry dish or pie plate and press with palm and fingers to cover the plate evenly.

PECAN WAFFLES & BLACKBERRY SYRUP

From the Roadrunner Roost B&B, Tomé

Waffle mix:

6 cups whole-wheat flour

3 cups all-purpose flour

2 cups instant nonfat dry milk

1 T. salt

1 cup sugar

1 cup wheat germ

$1/4$ cup baking powder

2 cups vegetable shortening

• In a large bowl, combine the dry ingredients, then cut in shortening and mix well. This makes enough batter for six servings.

Pecan waffle:

$2 1/4$ cups waffle mix (recipe above)

$1 1/3$ cups water

3 T. vegetable oil

3 eggs, separated

$1/2$ cup chopped pecans

• Preheat waffle iron. Beat egg whites until stiff, set aside.

• Combine waffle mix, water, oil, egg yolks, and pecans in a large bowl, then fold in egg whites.

• Serve with honey butter and homemade blackberry syrup (recipe follows).

Blackberry syrup:

5 cups blackberry purée, strained

6 cups sugar

1 cup corn syrup

4 T. lemon juice

• Boil to desired consistency, pour into $1/2$ pint jars, seal and water bath for 15 minutes. Makes 6 pints.

• BREADS & MUFFINS •

Nana Banana Bread, P. 70
From Casa de la Cuma, Santa Fe

Orange Almond Mighty Muffins, P. 59
From the High Feather Ranch, Cerrillos

ORANGE ALMOND MIGHTY MUFFINS

From The High Feather Ranch, Cerrillos

2 1/4 cups all-purpose flour
1/2 cup sugar
2 1/2 t. baking powder
1/2 t. baking soda
1/4 t. salt
1 cup sliced almonds

1/2 cup milk
1/2 cup orange juice
1/4 cup melted butter
1 egg
1 t. grated orange peel
powdered sugar

- In a large bowl, mix dry ingredients. Push mixture up sides of bowl to form a well.
- In a small bowl, combine liquids, butter, eggs and orange peel and beat to blend. Pour into well in large bowl and mix lightly.
- Spoon into 4 greased 6 oz. custard cups until heaping full. Place on a baking sheet.
- Bake at 375°F for 35 to 40 minutes.
- Let cool for 5 minutes, sprinkle with powdered sugar and serve.

MORNING GLORY MUFFINS

From the Chocolate Turtle, Corrales

2 cups flour

1 t. cinnamon

2 t. baking soda

1/2 t. salt

1 cup sugar

2 cups grated carrots

1 cup raisins

1/2 cup sweetened shredded coconut
   (optional)

1 cup chopped pecans

1 apple–cored, peeled and chopped

3 eggs

1 cup oil

2 t. vanilla

* Sift together flour, cinnamon, soda and salt in a large mixing bowl.
* Add carrots, raisins, coconut, pecans, apple and sugar.
* In a small bowl, beat eggs together and add oil and vanilla.
* Pour egg mixture into flour mixture and stir until well blended.
* Pour into muffin tins and bake at 350°F for 30 to 35 minutes or until golden brown and tops spring back when touched.

CHEESE BLINTZ MUFFINS
with blueberry sauce

From the Cinnamon Morning B&B, Albuquerque

1 lb. part-skim ricotta cheese

3 eggs

2 T. sour cream or yogurt

4 T. melted butter

½ cup biscuit mix

⅓ cup sugar

1 T. vanilla

• Mix together and bake at 350°F for 30 minutes (or until lightly browned) in greased muffin tins or minibundt pans.

• Place 2 muffins or 1 minibundt on plate and top with warm blueberry sauce (recipe below) and a dollop of sour cream. Makes 12 muffins or 1 minibundt.

For the blueberry sauce:

1 T. cornstarch

⅓ cup warm water

⅓ cup sugar

2 T. lemon juice

2 cups fresh or frozen blueberries

• Mix cornstarch and water, dissolve lumps. Add sugar, lemon juice and blueberries.

• Cook over medium heat, stirring until the mixture is thickened.

• Makes about 2 cups sauce.

MARGARITA MUFFINS

From the Cinnamon Morning B&B, Albuquerque

1 20-oz. can of crushed pineapple, drained

1 cup chopped pecans

¾ cup flaked coconut

1 cup sugar

2 cups flour

1 t. salt

1 t. baking soda

4 oz. light cream cheese, softened

1 mashed ripe banana

2 t. vanilla

1 beaten egg

1 6-oz. carton low-fat fruit yogurt, strawberry or peach

2 to 3 limes

powdered sugar to taste

* Preheat oven to 400°F.
* Spray a 12-cup muffin tin with Pam.
* Mix dry ingredients together in a bowl; add pecans and coconut and mix.
* In a separate bowl, beat together cream cheese, sugar, yogurt, egg, banana, pineapple and vanilla.
* Add wet to dry mixture, mixing lightly by hand.
* Fill muffin cups and bake for 20 to 25 minutes.
* While muffins are baking, mix the juice of 2 to 3 limes with powdered sugar. (The amount of powdered sugar can vary—you want a thin glaze).
* When muffins come out of the oven (slightly overbaked is best), remove and put in a shallow container and drizzle all of the glaze over the muffins; cover and let sit.

If baked the night before they will absorb all of the glaze. Serve at room temperature.

FAIRFIELD'S BREAD

From Rancho Arriba, Truchas

$1^1/_2$ to $1^3/_4$ cups all-purpose flour
    (some wheat germ can be substituted)

1 cup bran

1 t. baking powder

$^1/_2$ t. salt

$^1/_3$ cup sugar

$^1/_2$ t. ground cinnamon

$^1/_2$ t. ground clove

$^1/_2$ t. ground nutmeg

$^1/_3$ cup vegetable oil or butter

2 to 3 T. molasses

1 cup milk or water

$^1/_4$ cup fruit or nuts

* Preheat oven to 375°F. Combine dry ingredients in mixing bowl.
* In another bowl combine butter, molasses, milk, and fruit or nuts.
* Add wet mixture to dry mixture and knead with hands.
* Put dough in loaf pan and bake 20 to 30 minutes.

BANANA BLUEBERRY BREAD

From El Farolito, Santa Fe

$1/2$ cup butter, melted

1 cup sugar

2 eggs, lightly beaten

1 cup mashed ripe bananas

1 cup all-purpose flour

$1/2$ t. salt

1 t. baking soda

1 cup whole-wheat flour

$1/3$ cup hot water

$1/2$ cup frozen or fresh blueberries

$1/2$ cup chopped walnuts

* In a large bowl, combine butter and sugar. Mix in eggs and bananas until smooth.
* In a separate bowl, stir together all-purpose flour, salt, baking soda, and whole-wheat flour until blended.
* Add to banana mixture alternately with hot water. Fold in blueberries and walnuts.
* Spoon batter into a greased 9-by-5-inch loaf pan.
* Bake at 350°F for 1 hour and 10 minutes, or until toothpick inserted in center comes out clean.
* Cool in pan for 10 minutes, then turn out onto cooling rack.

LEMON MANGO GINGER BREAD

From El Farolito, Santa Fe

Batter

2½ cups all-purpose flour

1 t. baking powder

½ t. baking soda

1¼ cups sugar

½ cup butter

½ cup milk

3 eggs

½ cup lemon juice

⅛ t. lemon extract

½ t. powdered ginger

1 T. crystallized ginger, finely chopped

¾ cup mangos, diced and drained

Streusel

½ cup hazelnuts or pecans, finely chopped

¼ cup brown sugar

½ t. nutmeg

• In a medium bowl, stir together flour, baking powder and baking soda.

• In another bowl of an electric mixer, beat butter and sugar until creamy.

• Add eggs one at a time. Beat until fluffy.

• Beat in lemon juice and lemon extract followed by milk, powdered ginger and crystallized ginger. Add slowly to dry ingredients.

• Stir in mangos. Set aside.

• Stir together the streusel ingredients.

• Spoon ½ batter into well-greased loaf pan. Add ½ streusel, then the rest of the batter and top with the rest of the streusel.

• Bake at 350°F for 50 to 60 minutes, or until toothpick inserted in the center comes out clean. Cool before slicing.

PEAR WALNUT BREAD

From the Four Kachinas Inn, Santa Fe

3 cups all-purpose flour

1 t. baking powder

1 t. baking soda

1/4 t. salt

3/4 cup butter (room temperature)

1 1/2 cups sugar

4 eggs

2 t. vanilla extract

1 1/2 cups vanilla yogurt

1/2 cup brown sugar

1/2 cup walnuts, chopped

2 t. cinnamon

2 medium pears, diced

* Preheat oven to 350°F.
* Combine flour, baking powder, baking soda, and salt. Set aside.
* In the bowl of an electric mixer, beat butter and sugar until creamy.
* Add eggs one at a time. Continue to cream and add vanilla, then yogurt.
* Fold in all dry ingredients.
* Grease and flour two 9-by-5-inch loaf pans and then fill each halfway with batter.
* Combine brown sugar, walnuts, cinnamon and pears. Divide this mixture evenly between loaf pans to create a layer.
* Fill pans with remaining batter.
* Bake at 350°F for 50 to 60 minutes, or until toothpick inserted into the center comes out clean.

BANANA CRANBERRY BREAD

From Casitas de Gila, Gila

2 cups all-purpose flour
3/4 cup granulated sugar
3/4 t. baking soda
1/2 t. salt
1 cup cranberries (fresh or frozen)
3 ripe bananas

1/4 cup plain yogurt
2 eggs, beaten
1/3 cup butter, melted and cooled slightly
1 t. vanilla

* Preheat oven to 350°F
* Grease bottom and sides of a 9-by-4-by-3-inch loaf pan.
* Combine flour, sugar, baking soda, salt and cranberries in large bowl.
* Mash bananas until smooth. Combine bananas, yogurt, beaten eggs, melted butter and vanilla and stir thoroughly.
* Make a well in the center of the dry ingredients and add the liquid. Stir and fold with a rubber spatula until combined.
* Pour into loaf pan and bake for 60 minutes, or until top springs back when pressed. Turn out of pan onto a wire rack.

PUMPKIN NUT BREAD

From Casitas de Gila, Gila

2½ cups all-purpose flour

1¼ cups granulated sugar

½ cup light brown sugar

1 cup chopped walnuts or pecans

1½ t. baking soda

½ t. salt

1½ t. ground cloves

1½ t. ground cinnamon

1 t. ground nutmeg

1 egg

½ cup vegetable oil

15-oz. can pumpkin

• Preheat oven to 325°F.

• Toast walnuts or pecans if desired.

• Grease bottom and sides of a 9-by-4-by-3-inch loaf pan.

• Combine flour, granulated sugar, brown sugar, nuts, baking soda, salt, cloves, cinnamon and nutmeg in a large bowl.

• Beat egg in another bowl; stir in oil and pumpkin, then mix until smooth.

• Make a well in the center of the dry ingredients and add the liquid. Stir and fold with a rubber spatula until combined. Pour into loaf pan and bake for 60 minutes, or until top springs back when pressed. Turn out of pan and onto a wire rack.

MANDARIN MUFFINS

From Hacienda Vargas, Algodones

11-oz. can mandarin orange segments

1 well-beaten egg

1 cup sour cream

⅓ cup melted shortening

2 cups all-purpose flour

2 t. baking powder

½ t. salt

¼ t. baking soda

½ cup brown sugar, packed

¼ cup sugar

3 oz. cream cheese

• Drain mandarin orange segments, reserving liquid. Cut the segments into halves and place in measuring cup. Add reserved liquid to make 8 oz.

• Add beaten egg, sour cream and melted shortening. Set aside.

• Combine flour, baking powder, baking soda, salt and sugars in a large bowl.
Make a well in center of dry ingredients. Add wet mixture. Stir just until moistened.

• Spoon into greased muffin pans, filling halfway.

• Slice cream cheese into 12 pieces and place a piece on top of each muffin. Spoon more mixture on top of each muffin to ⅔ full.

• Bake at 400°F for 20 minutes.

NANA BANANA BREAD

From Casa de la Cuma, Santa Fe

2 cups all-purpose flour

1 t. baking soda

1/4 t. salt

1/2 cup butter

3/4 cup brown sugar

2 eggs, beaten

6 large, mashed, overripe bananas

1/2 cup nuts

1/2 cup Ghirardelli chocolate chips

* Preheat oven to 350°F.

* Lightly grease a 9-by-5-inch loaf pan, or 4 miniloaf pans.

* In a large bowl, combine flour, baking soda and salt.

* In a separate bowl, cream together butter and brown sugar. Stir in eggs, nuts and mashed bananas until well blended. Stir banana mixture into flour mixture; stir just until moistened. Pour batter into prepared loaf pan(s).

* Bake in preheated oven for 60 to 65 minutes (if using miniloafs, bake 40 minutes), until a toothpick inserted into center of the loaf comes out clean. Let bread cool in pan for 10 minutes, then turn out onto a wire rack.

PEACH BREAD

From the Water Street Inn, Santa Fe

3 cups flour

1 t. salt

1 t. baking soda

$1/4$ t. cinnamon

$1/4$ t. nutmeg

$1/4$ t. cloves

$1^3/_4$ cups sugar

$1^1/_2$ cups fresh or frozen peaches

4 eggs

$3/4$ cup oil

1 cup chopped pecans (optional)

* Mix flour, salt, baking soda, spices and sugar in large bowl.
* Mix remaining ingredients in small bowl.
* Stir together dry ingredients with fruit mixture.
* Grease and flour 2 large or 3 small loaf pans. Divide mixture evenly in loaf pans.
* Bake at 325°F for 1 hour, or until inserted toothpick comes out clean.

CHOCOLATE CHERRY MUFFINS

From the Grant Corner Inn, Santa Fe

2 cups all-purpose flour
$1/2$ cup sugar
$31/2$ T. unsweetened cocoa
1 T. baking powder
$1/2$ t. salt
1 egg
1 cup milk
$1/3$ cup vegetable oil
$21/2$ cups frozen tart cherries

- Preheat oven to 400°F.
- In a large bowl, mix flour, sugar, cocoa, baking powder and salt; set aside.
- In a small bowl mix egg, milk and oil.
- Make a well in the dry mixture and pour in the wet mixture; stir just until moistened.
- Fold in the cherries.
- Spoon into paper-lined muffin cups.
- Bake at 400°F for 20 to 25 minutes or until golden brown.

· SOUP & SALAD ·

Gazpacho, P. 83
From the Cinnamon Morning B&B, Albuquerque

Couscous Salad, P. 75
From the Bear Mountain Lodge, Silver City

COUSCOUS SALAD
with apricots, pine nuts & ginger

From the Bear Mountain Lodge, Silver City

1 cup instant couscous

1/2 cup water

1 cup fresh orange juice

1/2 cup light olive oil

2 T. champagne vinegar

8 dried apricots, thinly sliced, about 1/3 cup

1 T. dried currants

1 T. golden raisins

2 t. grated fresh ginger

1/2 t. salt

1/2 medium red onion, finely diced, about 1/2 cup

2 T. pine nuts, toasted

• Pour the couscous grains into a small mixing bowl.

• Combine the water, orange juice, olive oil, and 2 T. vinegar in a medium-size saucepan.

• Bring the liquid just to a boil and stir in the dried fruit, ginger, and 1/2 t. salt; pour immediately over the couscous.

• Cover the bowl and let it sit for 20 minutes.

• Bring a small pot of water to a boil and drop in the red onions for 15 seconds. Drain well; toss the onions with a few splashes of vinegar to draw out their pink color.

• When the couscous is ready, gently fluff it with a fork and toss with the pine nuts and onions.

• Add salt to season, and an additional splash of vinegar to brighten the flavor.

Serves 4

NATIVE AMERICAN STEW

From Apache Canyon Ranch, To'hajiilee

5 chile pods (stems and seeds removed, pods rinsed)

$1\frac{1}{2}$ lbs. of lean pork, beef or lamb (cut into bite-sized pieces)

$2\frac{1}{2}$ t. of salt

$2\frac{1}{2}$ quarts of water

2 medium, diced onions

4 cloves of garlic, minced

3 t. of garlic powder

3 cups of frozen corn posole (washed several times) or 2 cans of hominy

12- or 14-oz.carton of frozen red chile purée

chopped fresh cilantro or 1 T. of dried cilantro

⁕ Place chile pods, meat and posole into 8-quart pot of water, bring to a slow boil, cover and simmer 30 minutes.

⁕ Add onions, garlic, garlic powder, salt and red chile purée; add water if needed.

⁕ Bring to a slow boil again. Cover and cook over low to medium heat for $2\frac{1}{2}$ hours.

Serves 8 to 10

MIXED GREENS
with Gorgonzola, walnuts & red pear

From the Brooks Street Inn, Taos

8 handfuls of mixed greens

¼ red onion, thinly sliced

4 to 5 oz. crumbled Gorgonzola cheese
   at room temperature

1 red pear, slivered

1 cup toasted walnuts

¼ t. freshly ground pepper

6 to 7 T. virgin or extra virgin olive oil

2 to 3 T. raspberry vinegar (use vinegar
   with a fairly intense raspberry flavor)

Fresh raspberries for garnish

• To toast walnuts, preheat oven to 375°F. Place them on a baking sheet in a single layer and bake for 5 to 8 minutes until fragrant. Stir nuts a few times during baking and watch to make sure they don't burn.

• Select a variety of greens with different tastes, textures and colors (use mostly lettuces, but include chicory, arugula, lamb's lettuce or wild greens depending on the season). Wash and dry in salad spinner.

• Tear greens into bite-size pieces and place in salad bowl, then add sliced red onion.

• Grind pepper over salad and toss.

• Toss salad with oil and follow with vinegar, then toss again.

• Place equal amount of salad on salad plates. Top each salad with slivered pear, Gorgonzola, warm walnuts and a few fresh raspberries.

Serves 6 to 8

CASA BEAN SOUP

From Casa de las Chimeneas, Taos

1 cup dried navy or great northern beans

3 cups water

2 ham hocks, 1 cup ham, or 6 slices bacon, cooked and chopped

2 diced carrots

6 ribs celery with leaves, chopped

1 sliced onion

8 cups water

1 bay leaf

6 to 8 peppercorns

6 whole cloves

2 cloves garlic, chopped

1 cup freshly mashed potatoes (optional)

• Soak beans overnight in 3 cups water. Next morning, drain beans, place in large pot and add the rest of the ingredients. Heat another 30 minutes until carrot, celery and onion are soft.

• You may freeze the soup at this point. After reheated or thawed, remove any large hunks of meat and mince. Return to soup.

• Take a small amount of soup and pass through blender and return to pot. This binds the soup together nicely.

Makes 8 servings

CHILE & ORANGE VINAIGRETTE

From Casa de las Chimeneas, Taos

$1/4$ cup honey

$1/4$ cup canola oil

juice of one orange

$1/4$ cup tarragon vinegar

1 T. New Mexico green chile powder

- In a bowl blend with a whisk the honey and chile powder.
- Add the vinegar, blending well.
- Slowly add the oil. Then squeeze the orange while whisking. Add more chile powder if needed.
- Chill and serve with tossed salad.

Makes approximately 1 cup

BLACK BEAN CHILE SOUP
Mary Anne's recipe

From Casa del Granjero, Albuquerque

1 large yellow onion

1 t. chopped garlic

2 medium jalapeños

2 bell peppers (red or green)

8 to 10 fresh Roma tomatoes

15-oz. can of whole corn

15-oz. can of vegetable or chicken broth

2 15-oz. cans black beans

1 T. chile powder or chile mix

1 t. cumin

1 T. salt and black pepper

Fresh spinach

• Remove seeds from jalapeños and dice (wear gloves).

• Lightly brown onion and garlic in an 8-quart pot.

• Slice peppers into 1-inch squares, slice tomatoes into medium pieces and add with the rest of the ingredients except the spinach.

• Bring to a boil and simmer for 20 minutes.

• In a separate pan, wilt or steam the spinach leaves. Place wilted or chopped spinach in the bottom of soup bowls.

• Ladle in soup, serve with French bread.

Serves 6 to 8

GREEK MOUNTAIN SALAD

From Casa del Rio, Abiquiu

1 large or 2 medium tomatoes, sliced

1 red onion, thinly sliced

1 cucumber, peeled and sliced

$^1/_2$ cup or more calamata olives

$^1/_2$ cup cubed feta cheese

3 T. olive oil

3 T. freshly squeezed lemon juice

* Arrange tomatoes, onion, and cucumber in an attractive design on plate.
* Sprinkle feta, mint and olives over all.
* Mix olive oil and lemon juice together and drizzle on top or use only olive oil.

SWEET PEPPER SALAD
From Casa del Rio, Abiquiu

3 sweet green peppers
1 sweet red pepper
salt and black pepper to taste
1 T. freshly squeezed lemon juice
3 T. olive oil
1 or 2 cloves garlic peeled and crushed with salt in a mortar

* Place peppers directly on oven rack in center of oven and roast until they begin to pop and are brown.
* When collapsed and well roasted, place them in a large bowl and cover tightly with wet paper towels and a dish towel. Let steam for about 1 hour and then peel (using your fingers to separate the skin from the meat) and seed. Slice lengthwise into long strips.
* Place in a serving bowl.
* Mix lemon juice, oil and garlic and pour over peppers. Mix well.
* Serve with warm pita bread, Greek olives and feta cheese.

GAZPACHO

From the Cinnamon Morning B&B, Albuquerque

2 16-oz. cans tomatoes or fresh tomatoes

3 large cucumbers

3 large bell peppers

    (different colors are attractive)

4 cloves garlic

1 large onion

4 ribs celery

2 8-oz. cans black olives

3 zucchini

1 16-oz. jar diced pimentos

1 12-oz. can V-8 juice

1 cup wine vinegar

¾ cup olive oil

¼ cup salt

2 12-oz. cans lemon-lime soda

1 T. chipotle powder

Tabasco and Worcestershire sauce to taste

• Blend all vegetables together in a food processor; add all liquids and seasonings.

• Chill 24 hours before serving. Stores well.

Makes 18 servings

COLD AMBROSIA SOUP
From the Cinnamon Morning B&B, Albuquerque

2 medium-sized cantaloupes, peeled, seeded and cubed

1 6-oz. can orange juice concentrate

1 t. cinnamon

1/2 to 1 cup honey

1 pt. whipping cream

mint sprigs for garnish

• Purée cantaloupe in food processor or blender until smooth.

• Blend in remaining ingredients, adjusting honey to taste.

• Chill thoroughly and serve in chilled bowls or stemmed glasses.

• Garnish with mint sprigs.

• Other fruits such as peaches, mangoes and raspberries may be added as well.

Serves 6 to 8

ELLIS STORE GARLIC SOUP

From the Ellis Store Country Inn, Lincoln

6 heads fresh garlic

1 32-oz. can chicken stock

1 qt. heavy whipping cream

¼ t. cayenne pepper

¼ t. salt

1 cup bread crumbs (fresh or dried)

2 T. butter

2 T. olive oil

* Sauté garlic in olive oil and butter for 5 to 7 minutes. Do not brown.

* Add chicken stock; boil covered for 45 minutes.

* Add cream, salt, cayenne pepper and bread crumbs.

* Reheat, stirring until soup thickens. (You may add more bread crumbs to thicken soup.)

* Serve with croutons and sour cream, and add parsley for garnish.

* Keeps and intensifies for 5 days in refrigerator.

CELERY SEED DRESSING
From the Touchstone Inn, Taos

¼ cup sugar

⅓ cup light corn syrup

¼ cup balsamic vinegar

2 t. celery seed

1 t. dry mustard

1 t. salt

a sprinkle of white pepper (black pepper can be substituted)

1 t. of grated onion (onion powder can be substituted)

1 cup canola oil

• Combine all ingredients except oil. Beat with whisk.

• Add oil gradually and continue beating until the dressing thickens.

• You can serve this on anything from fruits to vegetables. It's a great marinade for chicken and fish, and it's splendid as a sauce for duck, too.

Ginger Pear Coffee Cake, P. 108

From El Farolito Inn, Santa Fe

Maggie's Wicked Apple Margarita, P. 89
From the Little Tree B&B, Taos

MAGGIE'S WICKED APPLE MARGARITA

From the Little Tree B&B, Taos

2 1/4 cups high-quality, gold tequila

1 cup Cointreau

6 1/2 cups plain apple cider (do not use apple juice)

1 t. vanilla extract

1 vanilla bean

1 or 2 cinnamon sticks

3 T. fresh lemon juice

• Combine ingredients in large pitcher and stir.

• Place in freezer 12 to 24 hours prior to serving.

• Stir every 4 to 6 hours or so.

To serve

• Dip rim of margarita glass in apple cider and then dip into small plate of raw sugar.

• Place glasses in freezer for 5 minutes.

• Repeat to get a firm sugared rim. Freeze again for 5 minutes.

• Scoop frozen margarita into glass. Garnish with cinnamon sticks.

Makes approximately 10 servings

HOT SPICED PEARS

From Alma del Monte, Taos

6 fresh pears, peeled, cored and halved or 1 can pear halves, drained

1 cup simple syrup or 1 cup syrup from canned pears

3/4 cup brown sugar

1 t. ground cinnamon

1/2 t. ground mace

* Place pear halves cut-side up in baking pan, pour in syrup.
* Combine brown sugar and spices, sprinkling evenly over pears.
* Bake at 350°F until heated through and glazed.
* Garnish with chopped pecans and a stemmed maraschino cherry. Serve warm.

Serves 6

SWEET POTATO PIE
From Apache Canyon Ranch, To'hajiilee

2 medium-large sweet potatoes (or 2 12- to 14-oz. cans)

2 egg whites

$1/2$ cup sugar

1 cup brown sugar

$1/2$ cup orange juice (fresh squeezed if possible)

1 t. vanilla (or orange extract)

$1 1/2$ t. nutmeg (or cinnamon)

$1/2$ orange rind for zest

9- to 10-inch pie shell

* Boil sweet potatoes until soft; peel and mash with hand mixer on low to medium speed.
* Mix egg whites and sugar and beat by hand until peaks are high.
* To potatoes, add beaten eggs, brown sugar, orange juice, nutmeg and orange zest.
* Mix until very smooth with hand mixer, pour into a pie shell.
* Bake at 375°F for 1 hour.

Serves 6 to 8

BLUEBERRY BUCKLE

From the Bear Mountain Lodge, Silver City

Cake:

1/4 cup butter

3/4 cup sugar

1 large egg

2 cups flour

2 t. baking powder

1/2 t. salt

1/2 cup milk

1 pt. blueberries

Topping:

1/4 cup butter

1/2 cup sugar

1/3 cup flour

1/2 t. cinnamon

* Preheat oven to 350°F. Line with waxed paper and grease an 8-inch springform pan.

* For the topping; mix all ingredients together in a food processor.

* For the cake; sift dry ingredients together in a bowl and set aside.

* Cream butter and sugar until fluffy.

* Add egg to butter mixture and blend until incorporated.

* Add dry ingredients to butter mixture alternately with the milk, starting and ending with flour.

* Fold in blueberries, and pour batter into the pan.

* Sprinkle topping over the cake, and bake for 1 hour.

COCONUT MACAROONS

From the Bear Mountain Lodge, Silver City

2 7-oz. packages flaked coconut
1 14-oz. can sweetened condensed milk
1 t. vanilla extract
1 t. almond extract
$1/2$ cup almonds, ground

* Preheat oven to 350°F.
* Combine coconut, almonds, sweetened condensed milk, vanilla and almond extract in a large bowl. Mix until well blended.
* Drop by heaping teaspoons 2-inches apart onto aluminum foil-lined cookie sheets.
* Bake 8 to 10 minutes, or until lightly browned around the edges. Immediately remove cookies from baking sheets and let them cool on racks.
* Store loosely covered at room temperature.

Makes 60 cookies

MEXICAN CHOCOLATE CAKE

From Casa de las Chimeneas, Taos

In a bowl mix:

1¼ cups flour

¾ cup sugar

¼ cup corn starch

½ t. baking soda

½ t. salt

3 T. cocoa

1 t. cinnamon

In a blender mix:

⅓ cup oil

1 t. vanilla

1 T. vinegar

¾ cup cold water

¼ cup brandy

• Sift dry ingredients together. Blend wet ingredients. Mix the wet into the dry until thoroughly blended.

• Pour into lightly greased (Pam) baking pan, either 8-by-9-inch or round.

• Bake at 350°F until toothpick inserted in center comes out clean.

• Cool in pan for 5 minutes, and then invert on rack to finish cooling. Cover with glaze.

Chocolate Glaze:

2 T. cocoa

1 T. vegetable oil

1 T. corn syrup

2 T. Kahlua

2 t. water

1 t. cinnamon

¾ cup powdered sugar

• Combine all but powdered sugar in a small saucepan and stir over medium heat until smooth and shiny. Using a spatula, gradually blend in powdered sugar.

VICTORIAN APPLE CAKE

From Casa del Granjero, Albuquerque

3 cups flour
1½ cups sugar
3 t. baking powder
4 eggs
1 cup vegetable oil
1 T. vanilla

¼ cup lemon or orange juice
dash of salt
4 Granny Smith apples, cored and
    thickly sliced
extra sugar, to taste
ground cinnamon

* Preheat oven to 325°F.
* In a large bowl, mix first 8 ingredients until well blended. The batter will be thick and heavy.
* In a well-greased and floured tube or bundt pan, spoon ¼ of the batter. Place ⅓ apple slices on top and sprinkle with cinnamon and sugar to taste.
* Repeat layering until all the batter and apples are used, finishing with the batter on top.
* Bake the cake for 1 hour and 15 minutes, or until toothpick inserted in the center comes out clean.
* Let the cake cool for 10 minutes. Remove from pan and cool on metal rack.
* You may add raisins and nuts to the apple layers for variation.
* This cake stays moist for several days and may be glazed with icing or left plain.

BREAD PUDDING WITH LEMON SAUCE

From Casa del Granjero, Albuquerque

1 lb. loaf unsliced French bread,
   cut into 1-inch cubes

3 cups milk

½ cup butter or margarine, softened

1 cup sugar

4 egg yolks

1 t. vanilla

1 T. cinnamon

1 large apple, peeled, cored and sliced

½ cup chopped pecans

* Grease an 8-by-8-by-2-inch pan, set aside.

* In a large bowl, combine the bread cubes and the milk. Let sit for 5 minutes.

* In mixer bowl, beat butter and sugar and cinnamon until fluffy. Beat in egg yolks and vanilla. Stir the egg mixture into the bread mixture until well incorporated.

* In prepared baking dish place ⅓ of the mixture; cover with apple slices and nuts. Repeat this last step ending with the bread mixture.

* Place baking pan in a larger pan filled to about an inch with hot water.

* Bake at 350°F for about 45 minutes or until center is set. Serve with lemon sauce.

Lemon Sauce:

* In a saucepan, combine 1 egg, 1 cup sugar and ¼ cup butter. Cook and stir until mixture thickens and begins to boil.

* Remove from heat. Stir in juice from 1 lemon and ¾ cup whipping cream. Cool slightly before serving.

MALPAIS COOKIES

From the Cimarron Rose B&B, Grants

1$1/4$ cups butter

2 cups sugar

2 eggs (free-range)

2 t. pure vanilla

$1/4$ cup water

$3/4$ cup cocoa

2 cups unbleached flour

1 t. baking soda

salt

2 cups rolled oats

$1/2$ cup oat bran

$1/2$ cup rolled barley

chocolate chips

• Mix all ingredients together in a large mixing bowl.

• Drop onto cookie sheet and bake at 350°F.

• Remove from oven when still soft, but not glossy. Store in airtight container as soon as cooled.

• Overbaking or leaving out in dry air will make these delectable, chewy morsels hard as the lava flows they're named for. If this happens, they make delicious coffee dippers.

EXTRA SPECIAL CARROT CAKE

From Casa del Granjero, Albuquerque

2 1/2 cups all-purpose flour

3 t. baking soda

1 T. cinnamon

1/2 t. salt

3 large eggs

3/4 cup vegetable oil

3/4 cup buttermilk

2 cups sugar

1 T. vanilla

8 oz. crushed pineapple, drained

2 cups grated carrots

3 1/2 oz. shredded coconut

1 cup coarsely chopped walnuts
    (approx. 4 oz.)

Buttermilk Glaze:

1 cup sugar

1/2 cup buttermilk

1/4 lb. butter or margarine

1 T. white corn syrup

2 t. vanilla

1/2 t. baking soda

Cream Cheese Frosting:

1/4 lb. butter or margarine

8 oz. cream cheese

2 cups powdered sugar, sifted

1 t. orange juice

2 t. grated orange peel

1 t. vanilla

* Preheat oven to 350°F.

* Grease a 13-by-19-inch baking pan or 2 9-inch cake pans, set aside.

* Sift dry ingredients together and set aside.

* In a large bowl, beat the eggs, and add oil, coconut and walnuts. Stir until well mixed.

* Pour into prepared pans and bake for 1 hour or until toothpick inserted in center comes out clean.

While cake is baking, prepare the buttermilk glaze:

* In a medium saucepan, combine all ingredients except vanilla and bring to a boil.
* Reduce heat and cook, stirring occasionally for 5 minutes. Remove from heat and add vanilla. The baking soda may cause this mixture to rise to the top of the pan–use a pan with sufficient room to accommodate the mixture. Do not leave the mixture unattended.
* As soon as the cake is removed from the oven, pour the glaze over the hot cake. Cool cake in the pan until all of the glaze is absorbed.
* Turn cake out of pan if desired. Cool completely and then frost.

For the cream cheese frosting:

* Cream together butter or margarine and cream cheese until fluffy.
* Add the rest of the ingredients and mix until smooth.

RAISIN OATMEAL COOKIES
with chocolate chips
From the Old Town B&B, Albuquerque

½ cup vegetable shortening

1¼ cups sugar

½ cup molasses

2 eggs

1¾ cups all-purpose flour

1 t. salt

1 t. baking soda

1 t. cinnamon

2 cups of oats (quick or regular)

1 cup raisins

½ cup chocolate chips

* In a large bowl cream ½ cup shortening with 1¼ cups sugar. Blend in ½ cup molasses and 2 eggs. Beat gently until blended.
* Sift flour with salt, baking soda and cinnamon. Add to above mixture.
* Stir in oats and raisins (mix some of the oats with the raisins first so they're well separated and spread nicely throughout the batter). Fold in chocolate chips.
* Drop by spoonful on slightly greased cookie sheet and bake in 350°F oven for 10 to 12 minutes.

Makes 2 dozen cookies

CIMARRON'S TRAIL COOKIES

From the Cimarron Rose B&B, Grants

1 cup shortening

1½ cups brown sugar

2 eggs

½ cup buttermilk

1¾ cups unbleached flour

1 t. soda

1 t. baking powder

4 shakes of salt (⅛ t.)

1½ t. cinnamon

1½ t. mace

1 cup rolled 7-grain cereal or oats

1 cup rolled barley

½ cup wheat germ

½ cup oat bran

raisins

chopped dried apples (or other fruit) for people and horses or chocolate chips for people only

* Mix all ingredients together in a large mixing bowl.
* Drop onto cookie sheet and bake at 350°F.

MEXICAN BREAD PUDDING
with Kahlua chocolate sauce
From the Cinnamon Morning B&B, Albuquerque

1 loaf of French bread

2 cups milk, half-and-half or whipping cream

1 round of Mexican chocolate,
    chopped coarsely

4 oz. semi-sweet chocolate,
    chopped coarsely

½ cup pine nuts, toasted
    lightly in a dry skillet

2 large eggs

¼ cup sugar

½ t. cinnamon

1 T. vanilla

* Dry bread for 12 hours or until firm, trim off the crust and cut into 1½ - to 2-inch pieces.

* In a medium saucepan over medium heat, stir milk often until steaming.

* Remove and add Mexican and semi-sweet chocolate; stir until chocolate melts.

* In a bowl, beat eggs, sugar, vanilla and cinnamon to blend. Stir in milk mixture, pine nuts and bread. Let stand until bread is saturated (20 to 30 minutes), stirring often.

* Scrape mixture into a buttered, shallow 2- to 2½ -quart casserole, covering tightly with foil.

* Set in a pan that is at least 2 inches deep and 2 inches wider than the casserole.

* Put on rack in 350°F oven. Fill bottom of pan to about an inch with boiling water.

* Bake for 15 minutes. Uncover and continue baking until pudding center is set (when bread feels slightly firm when pressed).

* Serve hot or warm with Kahlua chocolate sauce (recipe follows).

Kahlua Chocolate Sauce:

4 oz. semi-sweet chocolate, chopped

$^2/_3$ cup whipping cream

$^1/_4$ cup sugar

2 to 3 T. Kahlua

• Pour cream into heavy saucepan; add chocolate, stirring constantly; heat until chocolate is melted; add sugar; and continue to stir. Heat until mixture begins to boil.

• Remove from heat, whisk until smooth, stir in Kahlua.

• Cool slightly before serving.

PEACH SUNDAES
with bourbon-pecan sauce

From the Cinnamon Morning B&B, Albuquerque

1 T. fresh lemon juice

3 large fresh peaches; peeled

6 T. unsalted butter

$^1/_2$ cup firmly packed brown sugar

3 T. whipping cream

$^1/_2$ cup toasted pecan pieces

1 T. bourbon or brandy flavoring

1 pint vanilla ice cream

• Cover peeled peaches with lemon juice.

• Melt butter over medium heat, add brown sugar and stir until bubbly.

• Add cream 1 tablespoon at a time, stirring until thick and smooth, 3 minutes.

• Stir in peaches, pecans and bourbon or brandy; heat 1 to 2 minutes.

• Spoon over individual servings of ice cream.

PEACH FRANGIPANE TART

From the Cinnamon Morning B&B, Albuquerque

1 9-inch pie crust

2 T. flour

3/4 slivered almonds

1/3 cup sugar

3 T. amaretto

2 T. butter; at room temperature

1 egg

5 peaches

1/2 cup peach or apricot preserves

• Preheat oven to 450°F.

• Coat crust with 1 tablespoon flour. Arrange floured side down in 9-inch tart pan with removable sides. Trim edges. Pierce all over with fork. Bake until golden brown, about 10 minutes. Cool on rack.

• Reduce oven to 400°F.

• Finely grind almonds in a food processor. Add remaining 1 tablespoon flour, sugar, amaretto and butter, and purée. Add egg and process until well blended. Pour into crust. Bake until filling begins to brown and is springy to touch, about 15 minutes. Cool on rack. (Can be prepared 6 hours ahead. Let stand at room temperature.)

• Blanch and peel peaches. Cut into slices. Drain well.

• Combine preserves and 1 tablespoon amaretto in small saucepan. Bring to boil, stirring to melt preserves. Boil until slightly thickened, about 30 seconds. Brush some preserves over tart filling.

• Arrange peaches atop preserves in concentric circles, overlapping slices. Brush with remaining preserves. (Can be prepared 3 hours ahead. Let stand at room temperature.)

FIVE FLAVOR POUND CAKE

From the Cinnamon Morning B&B, Albuquerque

1 cup shortening

1/2 cup butter

3 cups sugar

5 eggs

3 cups flour

1/2 t. baking powder

1/2 t. salt

1 cup milk

1 t. vanilla

1 t. almond extract

1 t. coconut extract

1 t. rum flavoring

1 t. lemon extract

• Cream together shortening, butter and sugar until light and fluffy, then add eggs one at a time; continue beating with each addition.

• Add milk, flavorings, and dry ingredients alternately, mixing well.

• Pour into greased and floured tube pan and bake at 350°F for 1 to 1 1/2 hours.

• Let cook 15 to 20 minutes and remove from pan.

SOMETHING YUMMY
Liz's breakfast recipe
From the Country Club B&B, Roswell

2 cans crescent rolls

8 oz. cream cheese

1 egg

1 t. vanilla or 2 t. brandy

1 cup sugar

8 T. butter, melted

$1/4$ cup sugar

cinnamon to taste

$3/4$ cup pecans

⋆ Unroll 1 can crescent rolls in greased 9-by-13-inch casserole; do not press seams together.

⋆ Mix cream cheese with 1 cup sugar, egg and vanilla or brandy. Spread over crescent rolls.

⋆ Cover with next can of crescent rolls.

⋆ Pour melted butter over top.

⋆ Top with mixture of remaining sugar mixed with cinnamon and pecans.

⋆ Bake at 350°F for 30 to 40 minutes; and test center for firmness.

CHUNKY OATMEAL COOKIES

From Casa de la Cuma, Santa Fe

3/4 cup butter

1 1/4 cups packed light brown sugar

1/3 cup whole milk

1 large egg

2 t. vanilla

1 cup all-purpose flour

1/2 t. baking soda

1/2 t. cinnamon

3 cups slow-cooking oats

3/4 cup raisins or currants

1 cup chopped pecans

• Preheat oven to 375°F.

• Combine butter, sugar, milk, egg and vanilla.

• In a separate bowl, combine flour, baking soda, and cinnamon. Add oats and stir well.

• Pour dry mixture into the wet mixture and work with fingers until blended. Do not overwork. Work in raisins and pecans until just blended.

• Roll cookies into balls with the palm of your hand and flatten slightly, about 2 inches in diameter.

• Place cookies onto greased baking sheet about 2 inches apart. Bake for 13 minutes. Look at the edges–when they are brown, the cookies are perfect.

GINGER PEAR COFFEE CAKE

From El Farolito, Santa Fe

3 T. butter

2 fresh pears, peeled, cored and sliced

1/3 cup brown sugar

1 1/2 t. ginger

1 t. grated lemon peel

1 t. grated orange peel

1 egg

1/4 cup melted butter

1/2 cup milk

1 1/2 cups flour

1/2 cup sugar

1 1/2 t. baking powder

1/4 t. salt

- Preheat oven to 350°F.
- Place 3 tablespoons butter in 9-inch cake pan and melt.
- Arrange pear slices in bottom of pan in a spiral pattern.
- Mix brown sugar, ginger, lemon peel and orange peel; set aside.
- Beat egg, melted butter, and milk together.
- In a separate bowl, sift together flour, sugar, baking powder and salt.
- Stir egg and flour mixtures together until well blended.
- Pour batter over pears and spread evenly. Sprinkle brown sugar mixture over top. Cut through batter with knife to marble cake.
- Bake for 25 to 30 minutes. Let stand for 5 minutes. Invert cake onto serving plate.

BREAD PUDDING
with rum sauce
From the Ellis Store Country Inn, Lincoln

6 eggs

1 cup sugar

1 qt. heavy cream

3 t. cinnamon

$1\frac{1}{2}$ T. vanilla

6 cups broken bread pieces

* Preheat oven to 350°F.
* In a large bowl, mix the first five ingredients, then mix in bread pieces and pour into a buttered 9-by-12-inch Pyrex dish.
* Place this pan into a larger baking pan with about 1 inch of water; cover entire large pan with foil so that it will steam bake.
* Bake for 1 hour. Cool before placing in refrigerator. Will keep 6 days.

Rum Sauce for Bread Pudding:

1 cube butter

1 $\frac{1}{2}$ cups powdered sugar

1 qt. heavy cream

3 oz. spiced rum

6 egg yolks, beaten

* In a 2-quart pan, melt butter on low heat, and add cream and powdered sugar, stirring to dissolve.
* Add beaten egg yolks (add a little of the hot mixture to the eggs first).
* Heat rum in the microwave until it's the same temperature as the cream mixture. Turn off burner, add rum. Then heat on low heat, stirring until sauce thickens.
* Cool and place in glass jar. Will keep for 4 to 5 days.

APPLE CAKE

From the Four Kachinas Inn, Santa Fe

2 t. cinnamon

5 T. sugar

$1/4$ t. nutmeg

3 medium to large apples (Rome or
   Macintosh are good)

1 lemon

3 cups all-purpose flour

2 cups sugar

1 cup vegetable oil

4 eggs

3 t. baking powder

$2^{1}/2$ t. vanilla

1 t. salt

$1/4$ cup orange juice

• Preheat oven to 350°F.

• Mix together the cinnamon, sugar and nutmeg.

• Peel and core the apples and slice into small pieces. Squirt $1/2$ to 1 lemon's juice over the apples to taste. Sprinkle the sugar mixture over the apples. Set aside.

• To prepare batter, beat all other ingredients together until smooth. Pour $1/4$ of the mixture into a well-greased 9-inch Bundt pan.

• Arrange about $1/4$ of the apples around the pan, covering the layer of batter.

• Pour another $1/4$ of the batter and add $1/4$ more of the apples so that the apples will be mixed throughout the cake.

• Pour the remaining batter over the apples and top the batter with remaining apples.

• Bake for an hour or until golden brown. Remove from oven, even if it looks slightly underdone on top. Let stand for 5 minutes, then remove from the pan.

OATMEAL APRICOT COOKIES

From the Four Kachinas Inn, Santa Fe

1 cup sugar

1 cup brown sugar

1 cup butter

2 eggs

2 cups flour

1 t. cinnamon

1 t. baking soda

3 cups quick oats

2 cups chopped dried apricots

* In a medium bowl, mix wet ingredients together.
* Add dry ingredients to bowl.
* Drop by teaspoonful onto baking sheet. Bake at 350°F for 15 to 20 minutes.

Makes 30 cookies

CHOCOLATE MOUSSE
From High Feather Ranch, Cerrillos

12 oz. semi-sweet chocolate chips
1½ t. vanilla
¼ t. salt
1½ cups whipping cream heated to a boil
6 egg yolks
2 egg whites
whipped cream

• Combine chocolate, vanilla and salt in processor using steel knife and mix 30 seconds.

• Add boiling cream and continue mixing for 30 seconds more or until chocolate is completely melted.

• Add yolks and mix 5 more seconds. Transfer to bowl and allow to cool.

• Beat egg whites to stiff peaks. Gently fold into chocolate mixture.

• Place in wine goblets, cover with plastic wrap and chill.

• Serve with whipped cream dollop and a sprig of mint.

Serves 4 to 6

LAVENDER POUND CAKE

From Los Poblanos Inn, Albuquerque

1$1/2$ cups sugar

1$1/4$ cups butter

$3/4$ t. vanilla

6 eggs

$3/4$ t. salt

2$2/3$ cups white flour

2 T. lavender petals

• Cream butter.

• Add sugar and cream, then vanilla and eggs. When mixed, add salt, flour and petals until just mixed.

• Pour batter into a prepared loaf pan and bake at 325°F for about one hour. If it is getting too dark on top, turn the oven down to 300°F.

• Cool 10 minutes in pan, then remove from pan and while still warm.

• Brush top and sides with lavender syrup (recipe follows) until well saturated.

Lavender Syrup:

1 cup water

1 cup sugar

$1/2$ cup lavender petals

• Bring water and sugar to a boil.

• Once dissolved, take off heat and add petals.

• Let cool to room temperature, then transfer to an airtight container.

• Chill overnight, then strain. Syrup will keep for 2 months in refrigerator.

ORGANIC COFFEE CAKE

From Riversong Ranch, Taos

2 T. organic vegetable shortening
    (made by Spectrum)
$1/2$ cup of sugar
1 egg (or substitute), separated

$3/4$ cup whole-wheat pastry flour
2 t. baking powder
$1/4$ cup of milk
$1/2$ t. vanilla

• Cream shortening and sugar, add beaten egg yolk and sifted dry ingredients alternately with milk.

• Add vanilla.

• Fold in stiffly beaten egg white.

• Spread $1/2$ of the mixture in a deep greased pie pan.

Filling:
$1/2$ cup brown sugar
2 t. cinnamon

1 cup chopped walnuts
2 T. flour
2 T. melted ghee

• Mix all the ingredients thoroughly and spread half over the batter in the pie pan.

• Add the rest of the cake batter and then spread the remainder of the filling over the top.

• Bake at 350°F for 45 to 60 minutes.

CRANBERRY WHITE CHOCOLATE COOKIES

From the Little Tree B&B, Taos

¾ cup plus 2 T. butter

1½ cups sugar

1 egg

1½ cups all-purpose flour

1 t. baking soda

1½ cups rolled oats

1 cup white chocolate, chopped into small chunks

cranberries

* Heat oven to 375°F.

* In a large bowl, cream the butter, sugar and egg.

* In a second bowl, combine the rest of the ingredients.

* Add dry ingredients to wet; stir to combine.

* Add milk if necessary to reach a malleable consistency.

* Drop by rounded tablespoon 3 inches apart on cookie sheets.

* Shape 3-4 cranberries into each cookie.

* Bake 10 to 14 minutes; cool on wire racks.

* Serve same day or freeze.

Makes 60 cookies

ORANGE POPPYSEED CAKE

From the Madeleine Inn, Santa Fe

1/2 lb. butter

1 cup sugar

4 eggs

2 cups flour

2 t. baking powder

1/2 t. baking soda

1/8 t. salt

1 t. vanilla

2 cups sour cream

1/4 cup poppy seeds

1 t. orange rind

* Spray tube pan with Pam and preheat oven to 350°F.
* In mixing bowl, combine sour cream, butter, sugar and eggs until smooth. Add orange rind.
* In another bowl, combine flour, baking powder, baking soda and salt.
* Add this alternately with sour cream and butter mixture. Mix well, scraping sides of bowl well in between additions.
* Add poppy seeds and vanilla, and mix well.
* Pour into prepared pan and bake for 1 hour, or until toothpick inserted comes out clean. Cool 8 to 10 minutes in pan, then remove to platter.

CRANBERRY CORNFLAKE COOKIES

From the Water Street Inn, Santa Fe

1 egg

1 cup butter

1 cup sugar

1½ cups flour

1 t. baking soda

1 t. cream of tartar

2 cups cornflakes

½ cup coconut

¾ cup dried cranberries

* Preheat oven to 350°F.
* Mix all ingredients in large bowl in order given. Mix well.
* Drop by rounded teaspoon onto ungreased cookie sheet. Flatten with fork.
* Bake for 10 to 12 minutes.

Makes 2 to 3 dozen cookies

BLUEBERRY BREAD PUDDING

From Alma del Monte, Taos

1 lb. loaf cinnamon raisin bread

5 eggs

¾ cup sugar

1 t. vanilla extract

1 t. cinnamon

¼ t. nutmeg

1¾ cups milk

6 T. cream cheese

¾ cup frozen blueberries

6 t. butter

• Preheat oven to 325°F.

• Whisk together eggs, milk, sugar, vanilla and spices.

• Cut bread into ½-inch cubes, add to egg mixture. Distribute half the bread mixture evenly into 6 2-cup ramekins sprayed with Pam.

• Dot with cream cheese and blueberries.

• Cover each ramekin with remaining bread mixture and dot with butter.

• Bake until pudding is browned and set, about 45 minutes.

• To serve, remove puddings from ramekins and center on plate. Garnish with fresh blueberries or blueberry sauce and a dollop of whipped cream.

Serves 6

RASPBERRY FIZZ

From the Grant Corner Inn, Santa Fe

$1/2$ cup fresh or frozen unsweetened raspberries

$1/2$ cup apricot nectar, chilled

5 ice cubes

1 T. powdered sugar

$1/2$ t. lemon juice

$1/4$ cup chilled club soda

lime slices for garnish

- Blend raspberries, nectar and ice in a blender on high until smooth.
- Add powdered sugar and lemon juice and blend another 30 seconds.
- Stir in club soda.
- Pour into frosted, stemmed goblets and garnish with slices of lime.

Makes 2 servings

STRAWBERRY ORANGE SMOOTHIE

From Alma del Monte, Taos

2 cups fresh strawberries, cleaned, halved and frozen

2 cups fresh pineapple chunks

⅓ cup orange juice concentrate

8 oz. low-fat vanilla yogurt

* Process all ingredients in a blender until smooth.
* Garnish with a whole strawberry on edge of glass and serve immediately.

Makes 6 servings

RUSSIAN TEA
From the Lazy K Ranch, Edgewood

1 large can pineapple juice

1 small can frozen orange juice

1 small can frozen lemonade

2 small cans water

1 T. cloves in bag (empty a tea bag and use this bag to hold the cloves, tying it
with the string on the tea bag)

2 qt. water

4 tea bags

1 cup sugar (or a little more to taste)

* In a large pot, simmer the bag of cloves in 1 quart of water for a few minutes.
* In another pot, steep the tea in the other quart of water (boiling).
* Add all juices, the remaining water and tea to the clove water (large pot).
* Add sugar to desired taste and simmer slightly.
* Two cinnamon sticks may be added with the cloves.

Makes approximately 1 gallon

THE PERFECT MARGARITA
From Adobe Nido, Albuquerque

$1/2$ can of 12 oz. limeade frozen concentrate (save the other half for the next batch)

6 oz. tequila

6 oz. Controy Licor de Naranjas (triple sec or other orange liqueur is fine)

lots of ice–chopped ice is fastest

6 oz. warm water

Margarita salt

fresh limes

⬥ In a blender, first add ice, then the frozen concentrate, then the tequila to help melt everything and finally the Controy and warm water.

⬥ Blend until smooth. If it is too frozen to pour, don't spoon it out. If it is that cold it will give you that nasty freeze on your throat and spoil the "perfectness." Instead, add a little more water and blend some more. It won't hurt the flavor at all.

⬥ Cut lime into triangles and use to wet the rim of the serving glasses. Dip the limed glass top into the margarita salt to cover the rim. Pour the margarita, add a wedge of lime in the rim and be careful not to mess up the salt. Remember–it is the Perfect Margarita.

Serves 4

· INDEX OF FEATURED B&Bs ·

Stewart House B&B, Taos

Riversong Ranch, Taos

High Feather Ranch, Cerrillos

Los Poblanos Inn, Albuquerque

Bear Mountain Lodge, Silver City

The Little Tree B&B, Taos

Casa del Granjero, Albuquerque

Ellis Store Country Inn, Lincoln

Several of the b&bs originally featured in this book have closed or changed ownership. We have not listed those that have closed as of this printing. Visit www.nmbba.org or call 800-661-6649 to get the most up-to-date listing of the state's b&bs.

Adobe Nido B&B
1124 Major Ave. NW
Albuquerque, NM 87107
505-344-1310/866-435-6436
www.adobenido.com

Apache Canyon Ranch B&B
4 Canyon Dr.
Laguna, NM 87026 (To'hajiilee)
505-908-2220/800-808-8310
www.apachecanyon.net

The Bobcat Inn
442 Old Las Vegas Hwy.
Santa Fe, NM 87505
505-988-9239
www.nm-inn.com

Casa Cuma B&B
105 Paseo de la Cuma
Santa Fe, NM 87501
505-216-7516
www.casacuma.com

Casa de las Chimeneas
405 Cordoba Ln.
Taos, NM 87571
575-758-4777/877-758-4777
www.visittaos.com

Casa del Granjero
414 C de Baca Ln. NW
Albuquerque, NM 87114
505-897-4144
www.casadelgranjero.com

Casa del Rio
PO Box 702
Abiquiú, NM 87510
505-753-2035
www.casadelrio.net

Casa Escondida B&B
64 CR 0100, PO Box 142
Chimayó, NM 87522
505-351-4805/800-643-7201
www.casaescondida.com

Casitas de Gila
50 Casita Flats Rd., PO Box 325
Gila, NM 88038
575-535-4455/877-923-4827
www.casitasdegila.com

Chocolate Turtle B&B
1098 W. Meadowlark Ln.
Corrales, NM 87048
505-898-1800/877-298-1800
www.chocolateturtlebb.com

Cimarron Rose
689 Oso Ridge Route
Grants, NM 87020
505-783-4770/800-856-5776
www.cimarronrose.com

Cinnamon Morning B&B
2700 Rio Grande Blvd. NW
Albuquerque, NM 87104
505-345-3541/800-214-9481
www.cinnamonmorning.com

Cottonwood Inn B&B
HCR 74, Box 24609
El Prado, NM 87529
575-776-5826/800-324-7120
www.taos-cottonwood.com

Country Club B&B
400 E. Country Club Rd.
Roswell, NM 88201
575-624-1794/888-624-1794
www.countryclubnb.com

Don Gaspar Inn
623 Don Gaspar Ave.
Santa Fe, NM 87505
505-986-8664/888-986-8664
www.dongaspar.com

El Farolito B&B Inn
514 Galisteo St.
Santa Fe, NM 87501
505-988-1631/888-634-8782
www.farolito.com

El Paradero B&B Inn
220 W. Manhattan Ave.
Santa Fe, NM 87501
505-988-1177/866-558-0918
www.elparadero.com

Ellis Store Country Inn
PO Box 15
Lincoln, NM 88338
575-653-4609/800-653-6460
www.ellisstore.com

Four Kachinas Inn
512 Webber St.
Santa Fe, NM 87501
505-982-2550/800-397-2564
www.fourkachinas.com

Hacienda del Sol
109 Mabel Dodge Ln., PO Box 177
Taos, NM 87571
575-758-0287/866-333-4459
www.taoshaciendadelsol.com

Hacienda Vargas
1431 NM 313
Algodones, NM 87001
505-867-9115/800-261-0006
www.haciendavargas.com

High Feather Ranch
29 High Feather Ranch
Cerrillos, NM 87010
505-424-1333/800-757-4410
www.highfeatherranch-bnb.com

Lazy K Ranch B&B
27 Autumnwood Court
Edgewood, NM 87015
505-281-2072/877-281-2072
www.lazykranchbb.com

Little Tree B&B
226 Hondo Seco Rd., PO Box 509
Arroyo Hondo, NM 87513
575-776-8467/800-334-8467
www.littletreebandb.com

Los Poblanos Inn & Cultural Center
4803 Rio Grande Blvd. NW
Los Ranchos de Albuquerque, NM 87107
505-344-9297
www.lospoblanos.com

The Madeleine
106 Faithway St.
Santa Fe, NM 87501
505-982-3465/888-877-7622
www.madeleineinn.com

Old Taos Guesthouse
1028 Witt Rd.
Taos, NM 87571
575-758-5448/800-758-5448
www.oldtaos.com

Old Town B&B
707 17th St. NW
Albuquerque, NM 87104
505-764-9144/888-900-9144
www.inn-new-mexico.com

Rancho Arriba B&B
PO Box 338
Truchas, NM 87578
505-689-2374
www.ranchoarriba.com

Rancho Manzana
26 Camino de Mision, HCR 64, Box 18
Chimayó, NM 87522
505-351-2227/888-505-2227
www.ranchomanzana.com

Stewart House B&B
46 NM 150, PO Box 3020
Taos, NM 87571
575-776-2557/888-505-2557
www.stewarthousebandb.com

Touchstone Inn
110 Mabel Dodge Ln., PO Box 1885
Taos, NM 87571
575-758-0192
www.touchstoneinn.com

Water Street Inn B&B
427 W. Water St.
Santa Fe, NM 87501
505-984-1193/800-646-6752
www.waterstreetinn.com